teach®
yourself

instant italian
elisabeth smith

For over 60 years, more than
50 million people have learnt over
750 subjects the **teach yourself**
way, with impressive results.

be where you want to be
with **teach yourself**

The publisher has used its best endeavours to ensure that the URLs for external websites referred to in this book are correct and active at the time of going to press. However, the publisher and the author have no responsibility for the websites and can make no guarantee that a site will remain live or that the content will remain relevant, decent or appropriate.

For UK order enquiries: please contact Bookpoint Ltd, 130 Milton Park, Abingdon, Oxon OX14 4SB. Telephone: +44 (0) 1235 827720. Fax: +44 (0) 1235 400454. Lines are open 09.00–17.00, Monday to Saturday, with a 24-hour message answering service. Details about our titles and how to order are available at www.teachyourself.co.uk

For USA order enquiries: please contact McGraw-Hill Customer Services, PO Box 545, Blacklick, OH 43004-0545, USA. Telephone: 1-800-722-4726. Fax: 1-614-755-5645.

For Canada order enquiries: please contact McGraw-Hill Ryerson Ltd, 300 Water St, Whitby, Ontario L1N 9B6, Canada. Telephone: 905 430 5000. Fax: 905 430 5020.

Long renowned as the authoritative source for self-guided learning – with more than 50 million copies sold worldwide – the **teach yourself** series includes over 500 titles in the fields of languages, crafts, hobbies, business, computing and education.

British Library Cataloguing in Publication Data: a catalogue record for this title is available from the British Library.

Library of Congress Catalog Card Number: on file.

First published in UK 1998 by Hodder Education, 338 Euston Road, London, NW1 3BH.

First published in US 1998 by McGraw-Hill Companies, Inc.

2nd edition published 2003. 3rd edition published 2006.

The **teach yourself** name is a registered trade mark of Hodder Headline.

Typeset by Transet Limited, Coventry, England.
Printed in Great Britain for Hodder Education, a division of Hodder Headline, 338 Euston Road, London, NW1 3BH, by Cox & Wyman Ltd, Reading, Berkshire.

Hodder Headline's policy is to use papers that are natural, renewable and recyclable products and made from wood grown in sustainable forests. The logging and manufacturing processes are expected to conform to the environmental regulations of the country of origin.

Impression number   10 9 8 7 6 5 4
Year   2010 2009 2008 2007 2006

contents

If, like me, you usually skip introductions, don't! Read on! You need to know how **Instant Italian** works and why.

When I decided to write the **Instant** series I first called it *Barebones*, because that's what you want: *no frills, no fuss, just the bare bones and go!* So in **Instant Italian** you'll find:

- Only 379 words to say, well... nearly everything.

- No ghastly grammar – just a few useful tips.

- No time wasters such as 'the pen of my aunt...'.

- No phrase book phrases for when you have a tooth extracted in Tuscany.

- No need to be perfect. Mistakes won't spoil your success.

I've put some 30 years of teaching experience into this course. I know how people learn. I also know how long they are motivated by a new project (a few weeks) and how little time they can spare to study each day (½ hour). That's why you'll complete **Instant Italian** in six weeks and get away with 35 minutes a day.

Of course there is some learning to do, but I have tried to make it as much fun as possible, even when it is boring. You'll meet Tom and Kate Walker on holiday in Italy. They do the kind of things you need to know about: shopping, eating out and getting about. Tom and Kate speak **Instant Italian** all the time, even to each other. What paragons of virtue!

To get the most out of this course, there are only two things you really should do:

- Follow the **Day-by-day guide** as suggested. Please don't skip bits and short-change your success. Everything is there for a reason.
- If you are a complete beginner, buy the recording that accompanies this book. It will get you to speak faster and with confidence.

When you have filled in your **Certificate** at the end of the book and can speak **Instant Italian**, I would like to hear from you. Why not visit my website www.elisabeth-smith.co.uk, e-mail me at elisabeth.smith@hodder.co.uk, or write to me care of Hodder Education, 338 Euston Road, London, NW1 3BH?

Elizabeth Smith

how this book works

Instant Italian has been structured for your rapid success. This is how it works:

Day-by-day guide Stick to it. If you miss a day, add one.

Dialogues Follow Tom and Kate through Italy. The English of Weeks 1–3 is in 'Italian-speak' to get you tuned in.

New words Don't fight them, don't skip them – learn them! The Flash cards will help you.

Good news grammar After you read it you can forget half and still succeed! That's why it's good news.

Flash words and flash sentences Read about these building blocks in the **Flash card** section on page 92. Then use them!

Learn by heart Obligatory! Memorizing puts you on the fast track to speaking in full sentences.

Let's speak Italian *You* will be doing the talking – in Italian.

Spot the keys Listen to rapid Italian and make sense of it.

Say it simply Learn how to use plain, **Instant Italian** to say what you want to say. Don't be shy!

Test your progress Mark your own test and be amazed by the result.

Answers This is where you'll find the answers to the exercises.

▶ This icon asks you to switch on the recording.

Pronunciation If you don't know about it and don't have the recording go straight to page 16. You need to know about pronunciation before you can start Week 1.

Progress chart Enter your score each week and monitor your progress. Are you going for *very good* or *outstanding*?

Certificate It's on the last page. In six weeks it will have your name on it!

progress chart

At the end of each week record your test score on the progress chart below.

At the end of the course throw out your worst result – anybody can have a bad week – and add up your *five* best weekly scores. Divide the total by five to get your average score and overall course result.

Write your result – *outstanding, excellent, very good* or *good* – on your **Certificate**. If you scored more than 80% enlarge it and frame it!

Progress chart

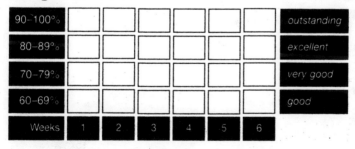

90–100%							outstanding
80–89%							excellent
70–79%							very good
60–69%							good
Weeks	1	2	3	4	5	6	

Total of five best weeks =

divided by five =

Your final result _____ %

01

week one

Study for 35 minutes – or a little longer if you can!

Day zero

- Read **Read this first!**
- Now read **How this book works.**

Day one

- Read **In the aeroplane.**
- Listen to/Read **In aereo.**
- Listen to/Read the **New words**, then learn some of them.

Day two

- Repeat **In aereo** and the **New words.**
- Listen to/Read **Pronunciation.**
- Learn more **New words.**
- Use the **Flash words** to help you.

Day three

- Learn all the **New words** until you know them well.
- Read and learn the **Good news grammar.**

Day four

- Cut out and learn the **Flash sentences.**
- Listen to/Read **Learn by heart.**

Day five

- Listen to/Read **Let's speak Italian.**
- Revise! Tomorrow you'll be testing your progress.

Day six

- Listen to/Read **Let's speak more Italian** (optional).
- Listen to/Read **Let's speak Italian – fast and fluently** (optional).
- Translate **Test your progress.**

Day seven is your day off!

In the aeroplane

Tom and Kate Walker are on their way to Italy. They are boarding flight QI 915 to Florence via Milan and squeeze past Gino Pavarotti. *(The English of Weeks 1–3 is in 'Italian-speak' to get you tuned in.)*

Tom   Excuse me, we have the seats 9a and 9b.

Gino   Yes, sure, one moment please.

Tom   Good day, we are Tom and Kate Walker.

Gino   Good morning, I am Pavarotti.

Tom   Luciano Pavarotti?

Gino   No, unfortunately. I am Gino Pavarotti.

Tom   We are going to Florence. Also you?

Gino   No, I am going to Milan. I am from Verona.

Tom   I was in Verona in April. Verona is very beautiful. I was in Verona for my company.

Gino   What do you do?

Tom   I work with the computers.

Gino   And you, Mrs Walker? What do you do? Where do you work?

Kate   I worked in a school for three years. Now I work at the Rover.

Gino   Are you from London?

Kate   No, we are from Manchester. We were one year in New York and two years in London. Now we are in Birmingham.

Gino   I worked for five years at the Fiat. Now I work at the Bank of Italy.

Tom   How is the work at the bank? Good?

Gino   The work is boring. I work too much but I need a lot of money. I have a big house, a Mercedes and four children. My wife is American. She has a girlfriend in Florida and telephones always. It costs a lot.

Kate   Now we are in holiday. Also you?

Gino   No, unfortunately. Not we are in holiday now. We are in holiday in August. We are going to Portofino but without children. We have a house there without telephone – and we go without mobile!

▶ In aereo

Tom and Kate Walker are on their way to Italy. They are boarding flight QI 915 to Firenze via Milano and squeeze past Gino Pavarotti.

Tom	Scusi, abbiamo i posti nove a e nove b.
Gino	Sì, certo, un momento per favore.
Tom	Buongiorno, siamo Tom e Kate Walker.
Gino	Buongiorno, sono Pavarotti.
Tom	Luciano Pavarotti?
Gino	No, purtroppo. Sono Gino Pavarotti.
Tom	Andiamo a Firenze. Anche Lei?
Gino	No, vado a Milano. Sono di Verona.
Tom	Sono stato a Verona in aprile. Verona è molto bella. Sono stato a Verona per la mia ditta.
Gino	Che cosa fa?
Tom	Lavoro con i computer.
Gino	E Lei, Signora Walker? Cosa fa? Dove lavora?
Kate	Ho lavorato in una scuola per tre anni. Adesso lavoro alla Rover.
Gino	È di Londra?
Kate	No, siamo di Manchester. Siamo stati un anno a New York e due anni a Londra. Adesso siamo a Birmingham.
Gino	Io ho lavorato per cinque anni alla Fiat. Adesso lavoro alla Banca d'Italia.
Tom	Com'è il lavoro alla banca? Buono?
Gino	Il lavoro è noioso. Lavoro troppo ma ho bisogno di molti soldi. Ho una casa grande, una Mercedes e quattro bambini. Mia moglie è americana. Ha un'amica in Florida e telefona sempre. Costa molto.
Kate	Adesso siamo in vacanza. Anche Lei?
Gino	No, purtroppo. Non siamo in vacanza adesso. Siamo in vacanza in agosto. Andiamo a Portofino ma senza bambini. Abbiamo una casa là senza telefono – e andiamo senza telefonino!

▶ New words

Cover up the Italian words, then say them OUT LOUD.

in aereo   *in the aeroplane*
scusi   *excuse me*
abbiamo   *we have*
il, la, i, le, l', gli   *the*
posti   *seats, places*
nove   *nine*
a, b   *(pronounced uh, bee)*
e   *and*
sì   *yes*
certo   *sure, certain*
un momento   *a moment*
per favore   *please*
buongiorno   *good day, good morning, hello*
il giorno   *the day*
siamo   *we are*
sono   *I am*
no   *no*
purtroppo   *unfortunately*
andiamo   *we go, we are going*
a   *to, at*
anche   *also, too*
Lei   *you*
vado   *I go, am going*
di   *from, of*
sono stato/a   *I have been, I was*
aprile   *April*
è   *is he/she/it...? he/she/it is, you are*
molto   *very, much, a lot*
bello/a   *beautiful*
per   *for*
il mio, la mia   *my*
ditta   *firm*
che?, che cosa?, cosa?   *what?*
fa   *you do/do you do?*
lavoro   *I work, I am working*
con   *with*
Signora   *Mrs, woman*

dove?   *where?*
lavora   *you work, he/she/it works*
ho; ho lavorato   *I have; I have worked, I worked*
un, una, un'   *a*
scuola   *school*
tre   *three*
anno, anni   *year, years*
adesso   *now*
al, alla   *at, at the*
siamo stati   *we have been, we were*
due   *two*
io   *I (only use to emphasize)*
cinque   *five*
la Banca d'Italia   *The Bank of Italy*
come   *how*
com'è? (come è)   *how is...?*
il lavoro   *the work*
buono/a   *good*
noioso/a   *boring*
troppo   *too much*
ma   *but*
ho bisogno (di)   *I need*
molti soldi   *a lot of money*
casa   *house*
grande   *big*
quattro   *four*
bambino/i   *child, children*
moglie   *wife*
americana   *American*
ha   *he/she/it has, you have*
amica   *girlfriend*
telefona   *she/he telephones*
sempre   *always*
costa   *it costs*
in vacanza   *on holiday*
agosto   *August*

senza *without*
là *there*
non *not*

il telefono *the telephone*
il telefonino *the mobile phone*

> **TOTAL NEW WORDS: 78**
> **...only 301 words to go!**

Some easy extras

These are all very similar to the English!

i mesi (the months)

gennaio, febbraio, marzo, aprile, maggio, giugno, luglio, agosto, settembre, ottobre, novembre, dicembre

i numeri (the numbers)

zero	uno	due	tre	quattro	cinque	sei	sette	otto	nove	dieci
0	1	2	3	4	5	6	7	8	9	10

More greetings

buona sera *good evening*, **buona notte** *good night*, **ciao** *hello/ goodbye*

Essential verbs for every day: 'to have' and 'to be'

In a couple of days you'll be reading about verbs in **Good news grammar**. Then on Day 3 spend ten minutes on these two verbs. I have put them into 'gift boxes' for you so you can't ignore them! But don't learn them today. Don't let's overdo it!

essere	*to be*	
(io)	sono	*I am*
(Lei)	è	*you are*
(lui)	è	*he/it is*
(lei)	è	*she/it is*
(noi)	siamo	*we are*
(loro)	sono	*they are*

avere	*to have*
ho	*I have*
ha	*you have*
ha	*he/it has*
ha	*she/it has*
abbiamo	*we have*
hanno	*they have*

▶ Pronunciation

The Italian language is beautiful, so drop all inhibitions and imagine that you are Italian! If Italian pronunciation is new to you please buy the recording. But if you are good at languages, or want a refresher, here are the rules:

First the vowels

The English word in brackets gives you an example of the sound. Say the sound and the Italian examples OUT LOUD.

a (*pasta*) vado, fa, casa, grande
e (*best*)   per, sempre, bella
i (*field*) il, si, amica, arrivederci
o (*not*)   no, non, sono, momento
u (*June*)   scusi, un, una, purtroppo

When you come across two vowels next to each other, as in euro, buono, or andiamo, say each one separately: e-u-ro, bu – o – no, andi – a – mo.

Consonants

There are only two which could be confusing: c and g. Each of these comes in a 'hard' and 'soft' variety, so you need to know when it is a hard sound and when it is soft.

Soft c:	This sounds like the ch in chocolate.
(c before e)	Either of these two produces a 'soft' sound.
(c before i)	**Examples:** certo, cinque
Note: cia, cio	Soft c, but the i is not pronounced. C(i)ao! Luc(i)ano, dic(i)otto
Hard c:	This sounds like the c in coffee.
c, ch	Either of these two produce the 'hard' sound. **Examples:** casa, cosa, scusi, che, chilo (*kilo*), cliente, credo
Soft g:	This sounds like the j in jet.
(g before e)	Either of these two produces a 'soft' sound.
(g before i)	**Examples:** Gino, Genova, viaggi
gia, gio, giu	Soft g, but the i is not pronounced. **Examples:** g(i)allo (*yellow*), g(i)orno, G(i)useppe
Hard g:	This sounds like the g in good.
g, gh	Either of these two produces a 'hard' sound. **Examples:** golf, grande, spaghetti, Inghilterra (*England*)

Special sounds:

Soft sc:	This sounds like the **sh** in ship.
(sc before e)	Either of these two produces a 'soft' sound.
(sc before i)	**Examples:** scena (*scene*), sci (*ski*)
h	This is always silent: **ho, ha:** say o and a!
gn	This sounds like the **ny** in canyon.
	Example: bisogno (say: 'bisonyo')
gl	This sounds like the 'lyer' sound in the word *million*: moglie (say 'mol-ye') **gli** (say 'lyee')
s	(between vowels) This sounds like the **z** in zombie.
	Examples: cosa, casa
	But at the beginning of a word, or before a consonant, it sounds like the **s** in sun: sì, scuola, costa, essere
z	This sounds like the **z** in zombie – but pretend there is a **d** in front of the z. (say: dzombie): agenzia, vacanze
Doubles:	Try to stretch these. Pretend there are four of them!
gg, ll, nn, etc.	bello, anno, mamma

Roll your 'r's!

Note that the Italian 'r' always has a clear rolled sound, unlike English.

favore, troppo, signora, Inghilterra

Which syllable to stress

You usually stress the last-but-one part of the word:

scu-si, ab-bi-a-mo, pos-ti, mo-men-to

But as always there are exceptions – sorry!

te-le-fo-na, cre-di-to

There is a written accent when the stress falls on the last vowel:

caffè (*coffee*), perché (*because*), lunedì (*Monday*)

and to differentiate between words spelt the same way.

▶ Good news grammar

This is the **Good News** part of each week. Remember I promised: No Ghastly Grammar! I simply explain the differences between English and Italian. This will help you to speak Italian **instantly!**

1 Names of things – nouns

There are two kinds of nouns in Italian: masculine and feminine. You can tell which is which by the word **il** or **la** (*the*), or **un** or **una** (*a* or *one*) in front of the word. You can also tell by the ending of the noun.

Most masculine nouns end in -o: **il lavoro, il telefono, un momento.**

Most feminine nouns end in -a: **la ditta, una casa.** The adjective describing the noun also ends in -o or -a. So the *good work* or *house* becomes: **il lavoro buono** or **una casa buona.**

When you talk about more than one thing (plural) the **il** and **la** change into **i** and **le**. And to complete the jigsaw, all words ending in -o and -a end in -i and -e in the plural.

   ...**i posti buoni** *the good seats*   **le case belle** *the beautiful houses*

This may sound complicated, but it is really easy, and you'll learn it without even noticing. If you get muddled and say 'il casa bello' or 'le vacanze buoni', Italians will still understand you perfectly!

Some nouns end in -e, so you can't tell what they are. In the **New words** they have **il** or **la** in front of them so you'll know.

The plural of -e is -i: **cane → cani** (*dog → dogs*).

2 Doing things – verbs

Unlike the English, the Italians do not use *I, you, he, she, it, we,* or *they,* to identify who is doing something unless they wish to clarify or stress it. So the only way you can tell who is doing something is by the verb itself. Each person has his or her own verb form or verb ending, but sometimes a verb or an ending is shared. This could lead to some confusion, but amazingly it usually works out all right. There are a few verbs which you'll use every day. I have put the first two in a box on page 15. Learn them now, it won't take long!

3 Asking questions

This is very easy. In Italian there is no difference between *Rome is beautiful.* and *Is Rome beautiful?* **Roma è bella. Roma è bella?** **Costa molto.** *It costs a lot.* **Costa molto?** *Does it cost a lot?*

Just use your voice to turn a statement into a question.

▶ Let's speak Italian

Here are ten English sentences. Read each sentence and say it in Italian – OUT LOUD! If you have the recording, listen to check your answers to **Let's speak Italian**.

1 Are you from London?
2 Yes, I am from London.
3 I am on holiday in August.
4 We are going to Como.
5 I was in Milan for my firm.
6 Do you have a Ferrari?
7 No, unfortunately.
8 We have a house in Rome.
9 How is the job with Fiat, good?
10 No, it is boring, but I need a lot of money.

Well, how many did you get right? If you are not happy, do it again.

Here are some questions in Italian. Answer these in Italian. Start every answer with sì and talk about yourself.

11 È di Manchester?
12 Ha una casa a Londra?
13 Andiamo a Firenze. Anche Lei?
14 Lavora in una ditta a Torino?
15 Il lavoro è buono?

Now tell someone in Italian...

16 ...that you have two children.
17 ...that you have been in Torino.
18 ...that you have a Fiat Punto.
19 ...that you need a girlfriend.
20 ...that Birmingham is boring in November.

Answers

1 È di Londra?
2 Sì, sono di Londra.
3 Sono in vacanza in agosto.
4 Andiamo a Como.
5 Sono stato (or stata) a Milano per la mia ditta.
6 Ha una Ferrari?
7 No, purtroppo.
8 Abbiamo una casa a Roma.
9 Com'è il lavoro alla Fiat, buono?
10 No, è noioso, ma ho bisogno di molti soldi.

11 Sì, sono di Manchester.
12 Sì, ho una casa a Londra.
13 Sì, vado a Firenze.
14 Sì, lavoro in una ditta a Torino.
15 Sì, il lavoro è buono.
16 Ho due bambini.
17 Sono stato/stata a Torino.
18 Ho una Fiat Punto.
19 Ho bisogno di un'amica.
20 Birmingham è noiosa in novembre.

Well, what was your score? For 20/20 take a triple gold star!

▶ Let's speak more Italian

Here are some optional exercises. They may stretch the 35 minutes a day by 15 minutes. But the extra practice will be worth it.

And always remember: near enough is good enough!

In your own words

This exercise will teach you to express yourself freely. Use only the words you have learned so far.

Tell me in your own words that...

Example you are Peter Smith
Sono Peter Smith.

1 you originate from Manchester
2 you have an American friend
3 you are a workaholic...
4 ...but you don't have a lot of cash
5 you have two children
6 the children are six and eight (have six and eight years)
7 unfortunately you work with PCs; the work is not interesting
8 your wife works in a bank
9 you own a property in Portofino
10 your children are in Birmingham

Answers

1 Sono di Manchester.
2 Ho un amico americano / un'amica americana.
3 Lavoro molto...
4 ...ma non ho molti soldi.
5 Ho due bambini.
6 I bambini hanno sei e otto anni.
7 Purtroppo lavoro con i computer; il lavoro non è interessante.
8 Mia moglie lavora in una banca.
9 Ho una casa a Portofino.
10 I miei bambini sono a Birmingham.

▶ Let's speak Italian – fast and fluently

No more stuttering and stumbling! Get out the stopwatch and time yourself with this fluency practice.

Translate each section and check if it is correct, then cover up the answers and say the three or four sentences fast!

20 seconds per section for a silver star, 15 seconds for a gold star.

Some of the English is in 'Italian-speak' to help you.

Good evening. I am going to Milan. You, too?
No, I work in Verona – for a bank. But I am going to Turin.
I am on holiday – without computer.

Buonasera. Vado a Milano. Anche Lei?
No, io lavoro a Verona – per una banca. Ma vado a Torino.
Sono in vacanza – senza computer.

How is Portofino? Is it (feminine) big?
No, it is not big, but it is interesting.
It is very beautiful and very expensive.
A house in Portofino, it costs a lot of money.

Com'è Portofino? È grande?
No, non è grande, ma è interessante.
È molto bella e molto cara.
Una casa a Portofino costa molto.

I have a girlfriend, Gina.
She has a house in Como.
Oh, excuse me. One moment, please, it is Gina.
She is always on the phone. 'Bye!

Ho un'amica, Gina.
Ha una casa a Como.
Oh, scusi. Un momento, per favore, è Gina.
È sempre al telefono. Arrivederci!

Now say **all** the sentences in Italian without stopping and starting.

If you can do it in under one minute you are a fast and fluent winner!

But if you are not happy with your result – just try once more.

▶ Learn by heart

Don't be tempted to skip this exercise because it reminds you of school... If you want to speak, not stumble, saying a few lines by heart does the trick.

Learn **Buongiorno** by heart after you have filled in the gaps with your personal, or any other information. Say **Buongiorno** aloud and fairly fast. Can you beat 40 seconds?

Buongiorno!
Buongiorno, sono...(name).
Sono di ....(place).
Sono stato/a* a...................(place) in ....(month).
Ho lavorato alla...(firm) per due anni.
Adesso lavoro alla..(firm).
Ho una casa grande a................................(place) e costa molto.
In agosto andiamo a..(place).
Com'è Firenze in aprile? bella?
*stato if you are male, stata if you are female

Test your progress

This is your only written exercise. You'll be amazed how easy it is! Translate the 20 sentences without looking at the previous pages.

1 Good morning, we are Helen and Jane.
2 I am from Rome, you too?
3 Where do you work now?
4 I was in Milan in October.
5 My girlfriend is in Italy for one year.
6 We always go to Pisa in June.
7 I worked at Fiat in May.
8 What do you do in London?
9 I work in a school but without money.
10 The big house in Bologna is for the children.
11 One moment please, where is Luigi?
12 Does the house have a (the) telephone? No, unfortunately.
13 Does the Ferrari cost a lot? Yes, sure, it costs too much.
14 How is the work in Italy, good?
15 Mario has a friend in an American firm.
16 We were in Como for three days.
17 We have (the) good seats in aeroplane.
18 I always have (the) boring holidays.
19 I need a beautiful wife, a Lamborghini and a lot of money...
20 He telephones now with a firm in London.

When you have finished, look up the answers on page 86 and mark your work. Then enter your result on the **Progress chart** on page 9. If your score is higher than 80% you'll have done very well indeed!

02

week two

35 minutes a day – but a little extra will step up your progress!

25

Day one

- Read **In Tuscany**.
- Listen to/Read **In Toscana**.
- Listen to/Read the **New words**. Learn 20 easy ones.

Day two

- Repeat **In Toscana** and the **New words**.
- Go over **Pronunciation**, if you need to.
- Learn the harder **New words**.
- Use the **Flash words** to help you.

Day three

- Learn all the **New words** until you know them well.
- Read and learn the **Good news grammar**.

Day four

- Cut out and learn the ten **Flash sentences**.
- Have a first go at **Let's speak Italian**.

Day five

- Listen to/Read **Let's speak Italian**.
- Listen to/Read **Learn by heart**.

Day six

- Listen to/Read **Let's speak more Italian** (optional).
- Listen to/Read **Let's speak Italian – fast and fluently** (optional).
- Go over **Non ho molti soldi...**
- Translate **Test your progress**.

Day seven is a study-free day!

day-by-day guide

In Tuscany

In Florence Tom and Kate hire a car and drive through Tuscany. They speak to Carla Rossi of 'Pensione Rossi' and later to Paolo, the waiter. *(The English of Weeks 1–3 is in 'Italian-speak' to get you tuned in.)*

Kate	Good day. Do you have a room double for one night and not too expensive?
Carla	Yes, we have a room a little small with bath and shower. But the shower is broken. Perhaps my husband it can repair.
Tom	Where is the room?
Carla	It is here on the left. Is it enough big?
Tom	It is a little small but not it is bad. How much costs it?
Carla	Only €40 for two, but no cards of credit! The breakfast is from eight to nine and half.
Tom	All right, it we take. But can we make breakfast at eight less a quarter? Tomorrow at eight and a quarter we would like to go to Portofino.
Kate	And excuse me, where can we drink something? There is a bar here?
Carla	There are two bars at five minutes from here. Not it is difficult. 30 metres on the right and then always straight on.

(In the bar)

Paolo	What would you like?
Kate	We would like a coffee and a tea with milk.
Paolo	Would you like also something to eat?
Tom	What is there?
Paolo	We have cake of apples or rolls.
Kate	Two rolls with ham, please.
Tom	The ham not is good.
Kate	The mine is very good.
Tom	The table is too small.
Kate	But the toilets are big and very clean.
Tom	The tea is cold.
Kate	But the waiter is very handsome.
Tom	Waiter, the bill please!
Paolo	€9.10, please.

▶ In Toscana

In Firenze Tom and Kate hire a car and drive through Toscana. They speak to Carla Rossi of 'Pensione Rossi' and later to Paolo, the 'cameriere'.

Kate	Buongiorno. Ha una camera doppia per una notte e non troppo cara?
Carla	Sì, abbiamo una camera un po' piccola con bagno e doccia. Però la doccia è rotta. Forse mio marito la può riparare.
Tom	Dov'è la camera?
Carla	È qui a sinistra. È abbastanza grande?
Tom	È un po' piccola ma non è male. Quanto costa?
Carla	Solo quaranta euro per due, però niente carte di credito! La prima colazione è dalle otto alle nove e mezza.
Tom	Va bene, la prendiamo. Però possiamo fare colazione alle otto meno un quarto? Domani alle otto e un quarto vorremmo andare a Portofino.
Kate	E scusi, dove possiamo bere qualcosa? C'è un bar qui?
Carla	Ci sono due bar a cinque minuti da qui. Non è difficile. Trenta metri a destra e poi sempre diritto.
(Nel bar)	
Paolo	Cosa desiderano?
Kate	Vorremmo un caffè e un tè con latte.
Paolo	Desiderano anche qualcosa da mangiare?
Tom	Che cosa c'è?
Paolo	Abbiamo della torta di mele o dei panini.
Kate	Due panini con prosciutto, per favore.
Tom	Il prosciutto non è buono.
Kate	Il mio è molto buono.
Tom	La tavola è troppo piccola.
Kate	Però i servizi sono grandi e molto puliti.
Tom	Il tè è freddo.
Kate	Ma il cameriere è molto bello.
Tom	Cameriere, il conto per favore!
Paolo	Nove euro e dieci, per favore.

▶ New words

Learning words the traditional way can be boring. If you enjoyed the flash cards why not make your own for the rest of the words. Always say the words OUT LOUD. It's the fast track to speaking!

camera *room*
doppio/a *double*
la notte *the night*
caro/a *expensive, dear*
un po', un pochino *a little, a very little*
piccolo/a *small*
bagno *bath*
però *but*
doccia *shower*
rotto/a *broken*
forse *perhaps*
marito *husband*
lo, la (by itself) *it, him, her, you*
può *he/she/it/you can*
riparare *to repair*
qui *here*
a sinistra *on the left*
abbastanza *enough*
male *bad*
quanto/a *how much...?*
solo *only*
niente *no, nothing, not anything*
carta di credito *credit card*
la prima colazione *the breakfast*
da – a *from – to/until*
dalle otto... *from eight o'clock* lit. *from the eight (hours)*
mezzo, mezza *half*
va bene *all right, OK*
prendiamo *we'll take*
prendere *to take*
possiamo *we can*

fare colazione *to have breakfast*
meno *less/before (with time)*
un quarto *a quarter*
domani *tomorrow*
vorremmo *we would like*
andare *to go*
bere *to drink*
qualcosa *something*
c'è *there is*
ci sono *there are*
minuto, minuti *minute, minutes*
difficile *difficult*
a destra *on the right*
poi *then*
diritto *straight on*
nel bar *in the bar*
il cameriere *the waiter*
cosa desiderano? *what would you like?*
il caffè *the coffee*
il tè *the tea*
il latte *the milk*
da mangiare *(something to) eat*
torta di mele *apple cake (cake of apples)*
o *or*
panino, panini *roll, rolls*
prosciutto *ham*
tavola *table*
i servizi *the toilets*
pulito/a *clean*
freddo/a *cold*
conto *bill*

**TOTAL NEW WORDS: 62
...only 239 to go!**

Some useful extras

i numeri (numbers)

11 **undici**	19 **diciannove**	60 **sessanta**
12 **dodici**	20 **venti**	70 **settanta**
13 **tredici**	21 **ventuno**	80 **ottanta**
14 **quattordici**	22 **ventidue**	90 **novanta**
15 **quindici**	23 **ventitré**	100 **cento**
16 **sedici**	30 **trenta**	200 **duecento**
17 **diciassette**	40 **quaranta**	1,000 **mille**
18 **diciotto**	50 **cinquanta**	

il tempo (time)

a che ora?	*at what time?*	**un'ora**	*an hour*
alle cinque	*at five o'clock*	**un giorno**	*a day*
è l'una	*it is one o'clock*	**una settimana**	*a week*
sono le due	*it is two o'clock*	**un mese**	*a month*
un minuto	*a minute*	**un anno**	*a year*

half past = and half	**e mezzo**
quarter past = and a quarter	**e un quarto**
quarter to = less a quarter	**meno un quarto**

▶ Good news grammar

1 *I, you, he, she, we, they*

In Italian these are: **io, Lei** or **tu, lui, lei, noi, loro**. But, as you know, they are only used for emphasis: *I do this, you did that.* **Lei** (*you*), as opposed to **lei** (*she*), takes a capital L. **Lei** is the formal and polite way of saying *you*. When in Italy and speaking **Instant Italian** use **Lei**. **Tu** (and its plural **voi**) is for family and friends, and requires a great deal more extra grammar. Next year!

2 Saying *non* (not)

Did you notice what happened to 'not' when Signor Pavarotti said:

Non abbiamo le vacanze adesso. *Not we have the holidays now.*

The 'not' moved in front of the verb. It does this all the time:

Il lavoro è buono. Il lavoro **non** è buono *The work **not** is good.*

3 Verbs – again

This week's good news: two more everyday verbs – *can* and *go* – in 'gift boxes', for easy learning. You'll need only a few minutes this time, because there is a bit of a pattern to each verb:

I usually ends in -o: **sono, ho, vado, lavoro**
you, he, she and *it* end in -e or -a: **è, ha, va, lavora,** but **può** (sorry)
we usually ends in -iamo: **andiamo, abbiamo, possiamo, prendiamo**
they usually ends in -ono or -an(n)o: **sono, possono, hanno, vanno**
Dead simple, isn't it?

Now learn **andare** and **potere**. Spend five minutes on each.

andare *to go*	
vado	*I go*
va	*you go*
	he, she, it goes
andiamo	*we go*
vanno	*they go*

potere *can*	
posso	*I can*
può	*you can*
	he, she, it can
possiamo	*we can*
possono	*they can*

More good news: there's a complete summary of verbs in Week 6 **Good news grammar** – if you get confused. Have a sneak preview! You'll know most of these in four weeks' time!

4 *C'è/ci sono*:   there is – is there?/there are – are there?

You will use this a lot, especially when asking questions.
   C'è un bar qui. Che cosa c'è? Ci **sono** servizi?
   C'è un cameriere molto bello?... Sì, sì...!

5 No collisions!

When two, usually identical, vowels meet, like **a+a** or **e+e**, one is dropped:
   un'amica (not una amica), **dov'è** (not dove è), **c'è** (not ce è)
More smooth talk!

6 *della, dei*

This is just a way of saying *some* cake or *some* rolls. Nothing too serious.

▶ Let's speak Italian

Now let's practise what you have learned. Here are ten English sentences for you to say in Italian OUT LOUD! After each sentence check to see if you got it right. If you didn't tick all ten, do the exercise again.

1 We would like a room.
2 At what time is there breakfast?
3 The telephone is broken.
4 How much is (costs) the room?
5 Where is the bar, on the right or on the left?
6 Is there something to eat?
7 All right, we take it.
8 Can we go to Florence?
9 We would like to go at half past two.
10 Excuse me, the bill please.

Now answer in Italian. Use **Sì** and speak about yourself.

11 Va alle otto e mezza?
12 Può mangiare un panino?
13 Ha una carta di credito?

Now answer with **No** and speak for yourself and a friend:

14 Ha una tavola per quattro?
15 Può riparare la Rover?
16 Va a Roma domani?

And now answer freely. Your answers may differ from mine but be correct.

17 Dov'è la pensione Rossi?
18 Com'è la camera?
19 Dove c'è un bar qui?
20 A che ora va a Milano Gina?

Answers

1 Vorremmo una camera.
2 A che ora c'è la prima colazione?
3 Il telefono è rotto.
4 Quanto costa la camera?
5 Dov'è il bar, a destra o a sinistra?
6 C'è qualcosa da mangiare?
7 Va bene, lo (or la) prendiamo.
8 Possiamo andare a Firenze?
9 Vorremmo andare alle due e mezza.
10 Scusi, il conto per favore.
11 Sì, vado alle otto e mezza.
12 Sì, posso mangiare un panino.
13 Sì, ho una carta di credito.
14 No, non abbiamo una tavola per quattro.
15 No, non possiamo riparare la Rover (or ripararla).
16 No, domani non andiamo a Roma.
17 La pensione Rossi è in Toscana.
18 La camera è un po' piccola ma non è male.
19 C'è un bar a dieci minuti da qui, a sinistra e poi sempre diritto.
20 (Gina) Va a Milano alle otto.

Did you get more than half right the first time? Have a gold star!

❏ Let's speak more Italian

Here are the two optional exercises. Remember, they may stretch the 35 minutes a day by 15 minutes. But the extra practice will be worth it.

In your own words

This exercise will teach you to express yourself freely.

Use only the words you have learned so far, and where possible answer using the verb form for 'we'.

Ask me in your own words...

1 if there is availability of a double room en suite
2 what the price of the room is for one night
3 where you can have (take) a coffee

Tell me...

4 that there is a café at 20 minutes from here; you go straight ahead
5 you would like (the) breakfast at 7.30
6 you are thinking of going to Portofino tomorrow
7 you would like two coffees and some cake of apples
8 what you don't like about the café (the table is too small and the cake isn't good)
9 what Kate likes about the café (the toilets are clean and the waiter is very handsome)
10 that the bill is €9.60

Answers

1 Ha una camera doppia con bagno o doccia?
2 Quanto costa per una notte?
3 Dove possiamo prendere un caffè?
4 C'è un bar a venti minuti da qui. Sempre diritto.
5 Vorremmo la prima colazione alle sette e mezza.
6 Vorremmo andare a Portofino domani.
7 Vorremmo due caffè e della torta di mele.
8 La tavola è troppo piccola e la torta non è buona.
9 I servizi sono puliti, e il cameriere è molto bello.
10 Il conto è nove euro e sessanta.

▶ Let's speak Italian – fast and fluently

No more stuttering and stumbling! Get out the stopwatch and time yourself with this fluency practice.

Translate each section and check if it is correct, then cover up the answers and say the three or four sentences fast!

20 seconds per section for a silver star, 15 seconds for a gold star.

Some of the English is in 'Italian-speak' to help you.

Good evening, do you have a room with bath?
80 euros is a little expensive.
We would like a room with shower.
How much is the breakfast? We can make breakfast at 7 o'clock?

Buonasera, ha una camera con bagno?
Ottanta euro è un po' cara.
Vorremmo una camera con doccia.
Quanto costa la prima colazione? Possiamo fare colazione alle sette?

Where is my house? Straight ahead, then to the right.
But we are going tomorrow to Pisa.
We would like to go at 9 hours and half.

Dov'è la mia casa? Sempre diritto, poi a destra.
Ma domani andiamo a Pisa.
Vorremmo andare alle nove e mezza.

The bar here is very small and very expensive.
But the coffee is good, and the rolls with ham are excellent.
The bill, please. How much? €38 for two coffees and two rolls?
We do not have enough money!

Il bar qui è molto piccolo e molto caro.
Ma il caffè è buono, e i panini con prosciutto sono molto buoni.
Il conto, per favore. Quanto? Trentotto euro per due caffè e due panini?
Non abbiamo abbastanza soldi!

Now say **all** the sentences in Italian without stopping and starting.

If you can do it in under a minute you are a fast and fluent winner!

But if you are not happy with your result – just try once more.

▶ Learn by heart

Learn the seven lines **Non ho molti soldi però… by heart**. Try to say them with a bit of 'drama' in 45–60 seconds! Choose one of these to fill the gap:

   mio marito, mia moglie, il mio amico, la mia amica.

Non ho molti soldi però…

Non ho molti soldi però vorrei* andare in Italia con …
Vorremmo andare a Portofino con la Rover.
È molto bello in aprile.
La pensione Rossi non è molto cara.
Quanto costa? Solo quaranta euro a notte.
Lo posso fare?
No. C'è sempre troppo lavoro nella mia ditta, e – la Rover è rotta!
*****vorrei:** *I would like to*

Test your progress

Translate in writing. What do you remember without checking back?

1 Where is there a telephone?
2 Excuse me, we only have a (the) credit card.
3 Can we eat at seven tomorrow?
4 Do you have a big enough table? We are (in) five.
5 The small rooms do not have a (the) bath.
6 We would like to eat ham and melon. **(melone)**
7 We can go from six to quarter to seven.
8 Where can we drink something?
9 We have been in the **(al)** bar from nine to half past ten.
10 All right, we take the Fiat for a day.
11 How much does the breakfast cost? Only €5.
12 Let's go and (to) repair the computer. It is broken.
13 How is the milk? Can the child drink it?
14 Where are the toilets, on the right or on the left?
15 Can I go to Hollywood – without my husband?
16 A coffee, please – nothing for you?
17 Where is (the) Signora Rossi? Perhaps in the **(nel)** bar?
18 €3.10 for a cold tea – it is a little expensive!
19 I have been in Tuscany in February. It is not bad.
20 There are 300 bars here, one at a hundred metres from here.

The answers are on page 87. The **Progress chart** awaits your score!

03

week three

Study for 35 minutes a day – but there are no penalties for doing more!

Day one

- Read **We are going shopping**.
- Listen to/Read **Andiamo a fare spese**.
- Read the **New words**, then learn some of them.

Day two

- Repeat **Andiamo a fare spese** and the **New words**.
- Learn all the **New words**. Use the **Flash cards!**

Day three

- Test yourself on all the **New words** – boring, boring, but you are over halfway already!
- Learn the **Good news grammar**.

Day four

- Cut out and learn the **Flash sentences**.
- Listen to/Read **Learn by heart**.

Day five

- Listen to/Read **Let's speak Italian**.
- Listen to/Read **Spot the keys**.

Day six

- Listen to/Read **Let's speak more Italian** (optional).
- Listen to/Read **Let's speak Italian – fast and fluently** (optional).
- Have a quick look at the **New words** from Weeks 1–3. You now know 218 words!... well, more or less.
- Translate **Test your progress**.

Day seven is your day off!

day-by-day guide

We are going shopping

Tom and Kate are near Portofino. They have rented a holiday apartment for a week. Kate plans to do some shopping... *(The English of Weeks 1–3 is in 'Italian-speak' to get you tuned in.)*

Kate   Today we must do the shopping. Let's go into the centre with the bus.

Tom   But there is bad weather, it makes cold and there is a lot of sport in television... the golf at two and half...

Kate   I am sorry, but we must first go to the cash dispenser and to the post office or to the tobacconist for the stamps... then into chemist's and into dry cleaner's.

Tom   In that case no golf... perhaps the football at four and a quarter... is it all?

Kate   No, we have to go in a big store to buy a suitcase new. Then I have to go to the supermarket and to the hairdresser's. And afterwards I would like to buy some shoes.

Tom   Bother...! Until when are open the shops?

Kate   Until seven and half, I believe.

Tom   Therefore no football... perhaps the tennis at eight.

(Later)

Kate   Hello Tom, here is the shopping: 200 grams of ham, a piece of cheese, half a kilo of apples, two kilos of potatoes, a mozzarella, sugar, bread, butter, some eggs, six beers and a bottle of wine. I have bought too much.

Tom   It doesn't matter. Yesterday not we have eaten much. And what is there in the bag big? Something for me?

Kate   Well... near to the UPIM there was a shop small and I have seen some shoes which were of my size. Not are they beautiful? White and blue. The sales assistant was very nice and handsome like Tom Cruise.

Tom   Who is Tom Cruise? And how much cost the shoes?

Kate   They were a very little expensive... but they cost the same in England... €100.

Tom   What? My wife is crazy!

Kate   But this T-shirt for the golf was very cheap. Size 42, only €10. Here is a newspaper English... and now not is there the tennis in television?

▶ Andiamo a fare spese

Tom and Kate are near Portofino. They have rented a holiday apartment for a week. Kate plans to do some shopping...

Kate	Oggi dobbiamo fare spese. Andiamo in centro con l'autobus.
Tom	Ma c'è brutto tempo, fa freddo e c'è molto sport in televisione... il golf alle due e mezza...
Kate	Mi dispiace ma dobbiamo prima passare al Bankomat e alla posta o dal tabaccaio per i francobolli... poi in farmacia e in tintoria.
Tom	Dunque niente golf... forse il calcio alle quattro e un quarto... è tutto?
Kate	No, dobbiamo andare in un grande magazzino per comprare una valigia nuova. Poi devo passare al supermercato e dal parrucchiere. E dopo vorrei comprare delle scarpe.
Tom	Uffa...! Fino a quando sono aperti i negozi?
Kate	Fino alle sette e mezza, credo.
Tom	Dunque niente calcio... forse il tennis alle otto.

(Più tardi)

Kate	Ciao, Tom, ecco la spesa: 200 grammi di prosciutto, un pezzo di formaggio, mezzo chilo di mele, due chili di patate, una mozzarella, zucchero, pane, burro, qualche uovo, sei birre e una bottiglia di vino. Ho comprato troppo.
Tom	Non importa. Ieri non abbiamo mangiato molto. E cosa c'è nella borsa grande? Qualcosa per me?
Kate	Beh... Vicino alla UPIM c'era un negozio piccolo e ho visto delle scarpe che erano del mio numero. Non sono belle? Bianche e blu. Il commesso era molto simpatico e bello come Tom Cruise.
Tom	Chi è Tom Cruise? E quanto costano le scarpe?
Kate	Erano un pochino care... ma costano lo stesso in Inghilterra... cento euro.
Tom	Cosa? Mia moglie è pazza!
Kate	Però questa T-shirt per il golf era molto conveniente. Taglia 42, solo dieci euro. Ecco un giornale inglese... e adesso non c'è il tennis in televisione?

▶ New words

Learn the **New words** in half the time using the flash cards.
There are 22 to start you off. Get a friend to make the rest!

fare spese *to do (the)
  shopping*
oggi *today*
dobbiamo *we must*
centro *centre*
autobus *bus*
brutto *bad, ugly*
tempo *weather* (also *time*)
fa freddo *it is cold* (used with
  weather)
la televisione *the TV*
mi dispiace *I am sorry*
prima *first*
passare a/da *pass, call on, go to*
da *from, by,* also: *at
  someone's house*
il Bankomat *name of cash
  dispenser*
posta *post office*
il tabaccaio *the tobacconist's*
  (sells stamps)
francobolli *stamps*
farmacia *chemist's, pharmacy*
tintoria *dry cleaner's*
dunque *therefore, in that case*
calcio *football*
tutto *all*
grande magazzino *department
  store*
comprare *to buy*
valigia *suitcase*
nuovo/a *new*
supermercato *supermarket*
il parrucchiere *the hairdresser's*
dopo *after, afterwards*
vorrei *I would like*
negozio, negozi *shop, shops*
le scarpe *the shoes*
uffa! *something you say when
  you are fed up, e.g. bother, damn*
fino a *until*

quando *when*
aperto *open*
credo *I think, believe*
più tardi *later*
ecco *here, here is/here are*
la spesa *the shopping*
grammi *grams*
pezzo *piece*
formaggio *cheese*
chilo *kilo*
patate *potatoes*
zucchero *sugar*
il pane *bread*
burro *butter*
qualche *some*
uovo, uova *egg, eggs*
birra, birre *beer, beers*
bottiglia *bottle*
vino *wine*
ho comprato *I bought, have
  bought*
non importa *no problem, it
  doesn't matter*
ieri *yesterday*
abbiamo mangiato *we ate,
  have eaten*
borsa *bag*
me, mi *me*
beh... *well...*
vicino, vicino a *near, near to*
la UPIM *well-known Italian
  chain store*
era/erano *was/were*
ho visto *I have seen*
bianco *white*
blu *blue*
commesso/a *sales assistant*
simpatico/a *nice*
chi *who*
costano *they cost*
lo stesso *the same*

Inghilterra *England*	**taglia** *size*
pazzo/a *crazy*	**il giornale** *the newspaper*
questo/a *this*	**inglese** *English*
conveniente *cheap*	

TOTAL NEW WORDS: 78
...only 161 words to go!

Some easy extras: *i colori* (colours)

bianco *white*	**nero** *black*	**rosso** *red*	**blu** *blue*
verde *green*	**giallo** *yellow*	**marrone** *brown*	**grigio** *grey*
arancione *orange*	**rosa** *pink*		

▶ Good news grammar

1 Doing more things with verbs: the past

Imagine you are getting married today! You would say 'I do.' If it happened yesterday, you would say 'I did' or 'I have done it'. To talk about something that happened before or in the past, in Italian you use *have* – which you know already – plus a slightly changed main verb.

So, **mangiare** becomes **mangiato** and **comprare** becomes **comprato**.

I bought, or I have bought	ho comp**rato**
you bought, or you have bought *he/she/it bought, or has bought* }	ha comp**rato**
we bought, or we have bought	abbiamo comp**rato**
they bought, or they have bought	hanno comp**rato**

And how about **mangiare?** How would you say: *We ate?* **Abbiamo mangiato!** Easy!...and **riparare?** How would you ask *Have you repaired?* **Ha riparato? Sì!**

Unfortunately you do not use *have* with all verbs. Here are a couple of 'rebels'.

essere *(to be)*	**sono stato/a**	*(I was, I have been)*
andare *(to go)*	**sono andato/a**	*(I went, I have gone)*

As you can see, **andare** (*go*) and **essere** (*be*) behave very strangely. Instead of *I have* you say *I am gone* and *I am been*.

| *Are you gone to Milano?* | **È andato a Milano?** |
| *No, I am not gone…* | **No, non sono andato.** |

No need to panic. By the end of Week 6 these two will be good friends.

2 Joining little words: turning two into one

Italians love their language to be smooth. Little pairs like *to–the*, *of–the* or *from–the* sound too 'staccato' to them so they 'melt' the two words into one. Here are six to give you a feel for them:

| a + il = **al** | da + il = **dal** | su + la = **sulla** |
| di + la = **della** | in + il = **nel** | con + il = **col** |

And if you don't 'melt'? No problem. Everyone will understand you.

3 *Passare da/a/in*

They all mean *to go to…*

Passo **dal** tabaccaio, passo **al** Bankomat, passo **in** farmacia.

Don't worry if you use the wrong one – nobody will laugh.

4 *Il mio, la mia, il suo, la sua*

When Italians say *my, your, his,* or *her* they always add *the*.

Il mio cane… la sua ditta… Sounds very grand, doesn't it?

Funnily enough, when you talk about your partner you simply say: **mio marito** or **mia moglie**. By the way, if you forget, it doesn't matter!

▶ Learn by heart

Say this dialogue in under one minute and with a lot of expression!

Dobbiamo fare spese… UFFA!

Tom   Oggi fa freddo. C'è il calcio in televisione.

Kate   Mi dispiace ma dobbiamo fare spese. Non abbiamo niente da mangiare. Dobbiamo prima passare al Bankomat e dopo al supermercato.

(più tardi)

Kate   Ecco la spesa! Ho comprato molto: prosciutto, formaggio, pane e burro, e – francobolli per l'Inghilterra.

Tom   Niente birre? niente vino? niente per me? Uffa!

▶ Let's speak Italian

Over to you! If you have the recording, use it to check your answers. Always answer OUT LOUD! Start with a ten-point warm-up. Say in Italian:

1 Now we must go.
2 I would like to do the shopping.
3 Are the shops open?
4 I am sorry, but it is too expensive.
5 Is there a bus for the centre?
6 We have eaten at Mario's.
7 Can we buy wine in the supermarket?
8 It costs €37.
9 We have been here from three to half past four.
10 Damn, the bottle is broken!

Answer in Italian using **No**. Speak about yourself.

11 Ha bisogno di un Bankomat?
12 Ha visto il calcio in televisione?
13 Ha comprato tutto in farmacia?

Answer in Italian using the words in brackets.

14 Cosa ha comprato? (niente)
15 Quando va al calcio? (oggi, alle due)
16 Fino a che ora è aperto? (fino alle nove)
17 Chi ha mangiato troppo? (noi)
18 Dove ha visto la valigia? (un negozio)
19 Ha comprato qui i francobolli? (no, alla posta)
20 Che tempo fa oggi? (brutto, freddo)

Answers

1 Adesso dobbiamo andare.
2 Vorrei fare spese.
3 Sono aperti i negozi?
4 Mi dispiace, ma è troppo caro.
5 C'è un autobus per il centro?
6 Abbiamo mangiato da Mario.
7 Possiamo comprare vino nel supermercato?
8 Costa trentasette euro.
9 Siamo stati qui dalle tre alle quattro e mezza.
10 Uffa! La bottiglia è rotta!

11 No, non ho bisogno di un Bankomat.
12 No, non ho visto il calcio in televisione.
13 No, non ho comprato tutto in farmacia.
14 Non ho comprato niente.
15 Vado oggi, alle due.
16 È aperto fino alle nove.
17 Noi abbiamo mangiato troppo.
18 Ho visto la valigia in un negozio.
19 No, ho comprato i francobolli alla posta.
20 C'è brutto tempo. Fa freddo.

▶ Let's speak more Italian

For these optional exercises add an extra 15 minutes to your daily schedule.

And remember, don't worry about getting the article or endings wrong. Near enough is good enough!

In your own words

This exercise will teach you to express yourself freely. Use only the words you have learned so far.

Tell me in your own words that...

1 you must go shopping today
2 you are aiming for the middle of the town
3 you are out of cash
4 you have to go first to an ATM...
5 ...then you have to go to the pharmacy
6 you saw a supermarket but it was not open
7 you have to buy black shoes, size 37
8 you bought the shoes, they were a bit expensive
9 you did not buy much in the supermarket
10 you bought bread, a piece of cheese and a bottle of white wine

---

Answers

1 Devo fare spese oggi.
2 Vado in centro.
3 Non ho soldi.
4 Prima devo passare al Bankomat...
5 ...poi devo andare in farmacia.
6 Ho visto un supermercato ma non era aperto.
7 Devo comprare delle scarpe nere, numero trentasette.
8 Ho comprato le scarpe, erano un pochino care.
9 Non ho comprato molto al supermercato.
10 Ho comprato pane, un pezzo di formaggio e una bottiglia di vino bianco.

▶ Let's speak Italian – fast and fluently

Translate each section and check if it is correct, then cover up the answers and say the three or four sentences fast!

20 seconds per section for a silver star, 15 seconds for a gold star.

Some of the English is in 'Italian-speak' to help you.

Excuse me, are you buying a television?
Is it expensive, the blue television?
No, not too much, in England it costs the same.

Scusi, compra una televisione?
È cara la televisione blu?
No, non troppo, in Inghilterra costa lo stesso.

We would like to buy a suitcase.
We have a suitcase but it (feminine) is too small.
I've seen a red suitcase but it is too expensive.

Vorremmo comprare una valigia.
Abbiamo una valigia, ma è troppo piccola.
Ho visto una valigia rossa, ma è troppo cara.

The weather was bad in April.
I was in Venice. I ate in the town centre.
The restaurant was very expensive – 300 euros.
The waiter wasn't handsome but he was nice.

C'era brutto tempo in aprile.
Ero a Venezia. Ho mangiato in centro.
Il ristorante era molto caro – trecento euro.
Il cameriere non era bello ma era simpatico!

Now say **all** the sentences in Italian without stopping and starting.

If you can do it in under one minute you are a fast and fluent winner!

But if you are not happy with your result – just try once more.

▶ Spot the keys

By now you can say many things in Italian. But what happens if you ask a question and don't understand the answer – hitting you at the speed of an automatic rifle? The smart way is not to panic, but to listen only for the words you know. Any familiar words which you pick up will provide you with **Key words** – clues to what the other person is saying.

If you have the recording, listen to the dialogue. If you don't – read on.

You   **Scusi, dov'è la posta per favore?**

An Italian   *È moltofacile,* **prima sempre diritto,** *finoalprossimoincrocio,* **dove c'è** *quel* **grande magazzino bianco. Poi a sinistra** *c'è una silo e una* **tintoria** *e proprio vicino alla* **banca c'è la posta!**

Can you find your way with the key words? I think you'll get there!

Test your progress

Translate in writing. Then check the answers and be amazed!

1 First, I would like to go to the cash dispenser.
2 In this shop the shoes cost too much.
3 Did you see my husband in the pharmacy?
4 We were here until a quarter past ten.
5 We saw the tennis in England, on (in) television.
6 I am sorry, we do not have the same in red in size 44.
7 This shop is not cheap.
8 Who repaired my telephone? You?
9 Here is the department store. But it is not open.
10 Today we did not buy too much, only bread and half a kilo of butter.
11 I ate everything – eggs, apples, potatoes and a piece of cheese.
12 We must do the shopping. Is this the centre?
13 Yesterday I was in the office until nine o'clock.
14 The English newspapers cost a lot in Italy.
15 Is there a bus? No? It does not matter.
16 He was a very nice sales assistant.
17 What is this? Something for us?
18 Did she buy the bag near here (here near) or at the UPIM?
19 Everything was very expensive. Therefore I did not buy anything.
20 We need three kilos I believe.

Remember to fill in the **Progress chart**. You are now halfway home!

04

week four

Day one

- Read **Let's go and eat**.
- Listen to/Read **Andiamo a mangiare**.
- Read the **New words**. Learn the easy ones.

Day two

- Repeat the dialogue. Learn the harder **New words**.
- Cut out the **Flash words** to help you.

Day three

- Learn all the **New words** until you know them well.
- Read and learn the **Good news grammar**.

Day four

- Cut out and learn the **Flash sentences**.
- Listen to/Read **Learn by heart**.

Day five

- Read **Say it simply**.
- Listen to/Read **Let's speak Italian**.

Day six

- Listen to/Read **Let's speak more Italian** (optional).
- Listen to/Read **Let's speak Italian – fast and fluently** (optional).
- Listen to/Read **Spot the keys**.
- Translate **Test your progress**.

Day seven

Are you keeping your scores above 60%? In that case... **have a good day off!**

day-by-day guide

Let's go and eat

Tom and Kate are back in Florence. Bruno Verdi invites them to dinner.

Kate Tom, someone has telephoned. He did not say why. Signor Verdi from Milan. Here is the number.

Tom Ah yes, Bruno Verdi, a good client. His firm is in Milan. I know him well, he is very nice. I have an appointment with him on Thursday. It is an important matter.

Tom *(Telephones)* Hello! Good morning Mr Verdi. I am Tom Walker... Yes, thank you... yes, sure, it is possible... of course... next week, very interesting... no, we have time. Wonderful! No, only two days... ah yes... when? Tonight, at eight... upstairs, by the exit... in front of the door... All right! In that case, until tonight, thank you very much, goodbye.

Kate What are we doing tonight?

Tom We are going to eat with Mr Verdi. In the centre, behind the church. He says that it is a new and very good restaurant. Mr Verdi is in Florence for three days with Edith and Peter Palmer from our company.

Kate I know Edith Palmer. She is boring and believes she knows everything. She has a terrible dog. Well... I believe I am sick. A bad cold and pains. I need a doctor.

Tom No, please. One cannot do that. Mr Verdi is very important.

(At the restaurant, Luigi, the head waiter, explains the menu.)

Luigi The fish is not on the menu and for dessert today there is tiramisu or some ice cream.

Bruno Mrs Walker, can I help you? Perhaps some pasta and afterwards meat?

Kate A steak with salad please.

Edith A steak, Kate? It is too much red meat!

Bruno And you, Mr Walker, what are you having? And what would you like to drink?

Tom A veal cutlet 'alla Milanese' with chips and vegetables, and a beer, please.

Edith There is a lot of oil in the vegetables, Tom.

······▶ Page 52

▶ Andiamo a mangiare

Tom and Kate are back in Florence. Bruno Verdi invites them to dinner.

Kate	Tom, ha telefonato qualcuno. Non ha detto perché. Il Signor Verdi di Milano. Ecco il numero.
Tom	Ah sì, Bruno Verdi, un buon cliente. La sua ditta è a Milano. Lo conosco bene, è molto simpatico. Ho un appuntamento con lui giovedì. È una cosa importante.
Tom	*(Telefona)* Pronto! Buongiorno Signor Verdi. Sono Tom Walker... Sì, grazie... sì, certo, è possibile... naturalmente... la settimana prossima, molto interessante... no, abbiamo tempo. Benissimo!... No, solo due giorni... ah sì... quando? Stasera, alle otto... su, all'uscita... davanti alla porta... Va bene! Dunque, a stasera, grazie mille, arrivederci.
Kate	Cosa facciamo stasera?
Tom	Andiamo a mangiare con il Signor Verdi. In centro, dietro alla chiesa. Dice che è un ristorante nuovo e molto buono. Il Signor Verdi è a Firenze per tre giorni con Edith e Peter Palmer della nostra ditta.
Kate	Conosco Edith Palmer. È noiosa e crede di sapere tutto. Ha un cane terribile. Beh... Credo di essere malata. Un brutto raffreddore e dolori. Ho bisogno del medico...
Tom	No, per favore! Non si può fare! Il Signor Verdi è molto importante.

(Al ristorante, Luigi, il cameriere, spiega il menù.)

Luigi	Il pesce non è sul menù e come dessert oggi c'è il tiramisù o del gelato.
Bruno	Signora Walker, posso aiutarla? Forse della pasta e dopo carne?
Kate	Una bistecca con insalata per favore.
Edith	Una bistecca, Kate? È troppa carne rossa!
Bruno	E Lei, Signor Walker, cosa prende? E cosa desidera bere?
Tom	Una cotoletta alla milanese con patatine e verdura, e una birra, per favore.
Edith	C'è molto olio nella verdura, Tom.

┅▶ Page 53

Bruno	And you, Mrs Palmer?
Edith	I take some chicken and a glass of water, please.
(Later)	
Bruno	Are we having fruit, or perhaps better – the tiramisu? No? Nothing? Have we finished? A coffee for someone? Nobody? Good, the bill, please.
Edith	Mr Verdi, please help me! How does one say 'doggy bag' in Italian? I would like a little meat for my dog.
Kate	But Edith, the dog is in England!

▶ New words

qualcuno *someone*

ha detto *he/she/it has said, you said*

perché *why, because*

signor *Mr, gentleman*

il cliente *the client*

il suo, la sua *his/her (agrees with noun)*

conosco *I know*

bene *well, also: good!*

appuntamento *appointment*

con lui *with him*

giovedì *Thursday*

una cosa *a matter, a thing*

importante *important*

pronto! *ready (and what you say when you answer the phone)*

grazie, grazie mille *thank you, many (a thousand) thanks*

certo *sure, certain*

possibile *possible*

naturalmente *of course*

la settimana prossima *next week*

interessante *interesting*

benissimo *very good, excellent*

su *up, upstairs, also on*

uscita *exit*

davanti a *in front of, before*

porta *door*

stasera *tonight*

facciamo *we do, make*

dietro a *behind*

chiesa *church*

dice *he/she/it says, you say*

che *that*

il ristorante *the restaurant*

nostro/a *our*

crede *he/she/it believes, you believe*

sapere *to know*

il cane *the dog*

terribile *terrible*

malato/a *sick, ill*

un raffreddore *a cold*

dolori *pains*

medico *doctor*

non si può fare *one can't do that, that's not on*

il pesce *the fish*

il menù *the menu*

come *like, as*

gelato *ice cream*

posso *I can*

aiutare *to help*

la carne *the meat*

bistecca *steak*

insalata *salad*

prende *you take, he/she/it takes*

desidera *you would like,*

Bruno	E Lei, Signora Palmer?
Edith	Prendo del pollo e un bicchiere d'acqua, per favore.
(Più tardi)	
Bruno	Prendiamo della frutta, o forse meglio – il tiramisù? No? Niente? Abbiamo finito? Un caffè per qualcuno? Nessuno? Bene, il conto, per favore!
Edith	Signor Verdi, mi aiuti per favore! Come si dice in italiano 'doggy bag'? Vorrei un po' di carne per il mio cane.
Kate	Ma Edith, il cane è in Inghilterra!

he/she/it would like
cotoletta alla milanese *veal cutlet 'alla milanese'*
le patatine *the chips*
verdura *vegetables*
olio *oil*
prendo *I take*
pollo *chicken*
il bicchiere *the glass*

acqua *water*
frutta *fruit*
meglio *better*
finito *finished*
nessuno *nobody*
mi aiuti, per favore *help me, please*
come si dice in italiano? *how do you say … in Italian?*

TOTAL NEW WORDS: 67
…only 94 words to go!

Last easy extras

The days of the week: *i giorni della settimana*

lunedì *Monday*
martedì *Tuesday*
mercoledì *Wednesday*
giovedì *Thursday*

venerdì *Friday*
sabato *Saturday*
domenica *Sunday*

▶ Good news grammar

1 The past: team players and rebels

Remember **comprare, mangiare** and **riparare**: they all end in **-are**?
Let's call them team players, because when you use them in the
past, to say that you *did* or *have done* something, they all end in
-ato.

...Ho compr**ato**/mangi**ato**/ripar**ato.**

Here are three more team players:

lavorare	→	lavor**ato**
aiutare	→	aiut**ato**
telefonare	→	telefon**ato**

Then there are a couple of players from a neighbouring team.
They end in **-ere** and finish up with **-uto** in the past.

conoscere	*(to know)*	→	conosci**uto**	*(known)*
credere	*(to believe)*	→	cred**uto**	*(believed)*

Finally the rebels: relax, there are only five.

dire	*(to say)*	→	**detto**	*(said)*
prendere	*(to take)*	→	**preso**	*(taken)*
fare	*(to do)*	→	**fatto**	*(done)*
vedere	*(to see)*	→	**visto**	*(seen)*
scrivere	*(to write)*	→	**scritto**	*(written)*

Spend 10 minutes practising these past forms. It's quite simple
once you use them.

Chi lo ha **detto**? Cosa ha **preso**? Cosa ha **fatto**?
Ha **visto** Luigi? Ho **scritto** a Maria.

Remember, if you ever 'lose' a verb or verb form, you'll find it
in the verb summary, page 80.

2 'It' and 'them'

Imagine you are talking about things – *wine, the company,
holidays* or *seats on the plane.* Now imagine you are referring
to these things. You would say *it* or *them.*

In Italian *it* is **lo** or **la**, and *them* is **li** or **le**, depending on whether
the things you are referring to are masculine or feminine, or one
thing or more.

Compro **vino**	**lo** compro	*I buy it*
Compra **la ditta**	**la** compra	*You/he/she/buys it*
Ha **le vacanze** in aprile	**le** ha in aprile	*he has them in April*
Abbiamo **posti**	**li** abbiamo	*we have them*

Did you notice?... The *it* or *them* always goes in front of the verb.

It I buy. It you buy. **Them** *we have.*

3 Last quick verb box – *dovere*: must, have to

Three minutes should do it, now you know the pattern.

> devo – deve – dobbiamo – devono

▶ Learn by heart

Here is a short piece about someone who is rather fed up. Put yourself in his shoes. Learn it and act it out in under 50 seconds.

Non mi piace...

A Conosce il Signor Martini?

  Ha telefonato ieri. Devo andare a mangiare con lui.

B Perché?

A È un buon cliente della ditta.

  Però non è simpatico – mangia e beve troppo.

B E quando?

A Stasera! C'è il calcio in televisione.

  Vorrei dire che sono malato... ma non posso...

  Sempre la ditta...!

B Ah... mi dispiace!

Say it simply

When people want to speak Italian but don't dare, it's usually because they are trying to *translate* what they want to say from English into Italian. But because they don't know some of the words they give up!

With **Instant Italian** you work around the words you don't know with the words you do know! And believe me, around 400 words are enough to say anything!

It may not always be very elegant, but who cares? You are speaking, *communicating!*

Here are three examples, showing you how to say things in a simple way. The English words which are not part of the **Instant** vocabulary have been highlighted.

1 You need to **change your flight** to London from Tuesday to Friday.

This is what you could say – simply:

Non possiamo andare martedì, vorremmo andare venerdì.
or:
Martedì non va bene per noi. Venerdì è meglio.

2 You want to get your **purse** from the coach which the driver has locked.

Say it simply:

Mi dispiace. I miei soldi sono sull'autobus.
or:
Ho bisogno di qualcosa importante. Mi dispiace molto, ma tutto è sull'autobus.

3 This time your friend has **just broken** the **heel** of her only pair of shoes. You have to catch a train and **need some help now**. This is what you could say:

Scusi, la scarpa è rotta, e abbiamo poco tempo. C'è un negozio qui dove riparano le scarpe al momento?

▶ Let's speak Italian

Here are eight sentences to say in Italian, and then on to greater things!

   1 I am sorry, I do not have time.
   2 Are we going with him?
   3 I would like a salad.
   4 We have been here yesterday.
   5 Excuse me, what did you say?
   6 I did not take this.
   7 When did you work in Italy?
   8 We did not do anything.

Now pretend you are in Italy with English friends who do not speak Italian. They will want you to ask people things and will want **you** to do it for them in Italian. They will say: 'Please ask him...' Start with **Scusi...**

   9 ...if he has seen Mr Rossi.
   10 ...where he bought the stamps.
   11 ...if he has an appointment now.
   12 ...where the restaurant is.

Now your friends will ask you to *tell* someone things. They use some words which you don't know, so you have to use your **Instant** words. They will say: 'Please tell her that...' Start your sentence with **Mi dispiace, ma...**

   13 ...her pasta is cold.
   14 ...we are not having wine, only water.
   15 ...she is a vegetarian.
   16 ...he does not have his number.

While shopping you are offered various items. You take them all, saying 'yes, I take it' or 'yes, I take them'.

   17 ...e la frutta?   **19** ...e le birre?
   18 ...e i gelati?   **20** ...e il vino?

Answers

   1 Mi dispiace, non ho tempo.
   2 Andiamo con lui?
   3 Vorrei un'insalata.
   4 Siamo stati (*or* state) qui ieri.
   5 Scusi, cosa ha detto?
   6 Non ho preso questo.
   7 Quando ha lavorato in Italia?
   8 Non abbiamo fatto niente.
   9 Scusi, ha visto il Signor Rossi?
   10 Scusi, dove ha comprato i francobolli?
   11 Scusi, ha un appuntamento adesso?
   12 Scusi, dov'è il ristorante?
   13 Mi dispiace, ma la sua pasta è fredda.
   14 Mi dispiace, ma non abbiamo vino, solo acqua.
   15 Mi dispiace, ma non mangia carne.
   16 Mi dispiace, ma non ha il suo numero.
   17 Sì, la prendo.
   18 Sì, li prendo.
   19 Sì, le prendo.
   20 Sì, lo prendo.

▶ Let's speak more Italian

In your own words

This exercise will teach you to express yourself freely. Use only the words you have learned so far. Where possible speak for yourself and a friend.

Tell me in your own words that...

1 somebody telephoned – it was Mr Verdi
2 you have an appointment with him next week
3 he works for a firm in Milan
4 he is a good client
5 you (plural) are going to eat in a new restaurant
6 you've got a bad cold – you need a doctor
7 you haven't got time to go to the doctor
8 you can go to the chemist
9 you'd like a steak with potatoes and salad
10 you went home at half past eleven

Answers

1 Ha telefonato qualcuno – era il Signor Verdi.
2 Ho un appuntamento con lui la settimana prossima.
3 Lavora per una ditta a Milano.
4 È un buon cliente.
5 Andiamo a mangiare in un ristorante nuovo.
6 Ho un brutto raffreddore – ho bisogno del medico.
7 Non abbiamo tempo di andare dal medico.
8 Possiamo andare in farmacia.
9 Vorrei una bistecca con patate e insalata.
10 Siamo andati a casa alle undici e mezza.

◘ Let's speak Italian – fast and fluently

Translate each section and check if it is correct, then cover up the answers and say the three or four sentences fast!

20 seconds per section for a silver star, 15 seconds for a gold star.

Some of the English is in 'Italian-speak' to help you.

Do you know Bruno Verdi? He phoned yesterday.
Why? He said it was important.
The appointment in Florence was on Wednesday.

Conosce Bruno Verdi? Ha telefonato ieri.
Perché? Ha detto che era importante.
L'appuntamento a Firenze era mercoledì.

Bruno is in Florence for three days.
There is a very good restaurant behind the church.
Bruno says it's expensive.

Bruno è a Firenze per tre giorni.
C'è un ristorante molto buono dietro alla chiesa.
Bruno dice che è caro.

Unfortunately, I can't go to the restaurant.
My dog is ill. He has eaten too much meat.
Oh, I am very sorry. How do you say in Italian: 'Poor little thing?'
(*poveretto*)

Purtroppo, non posso andare al ristorante.
Il mio cane è malato. Ha mangiato troppa carne.
Oh, mi dispiace. Come si dice in italiano 'Poor little thing'?
'Poveretto.'

Now say **all** the sentences in Italian without stopping and starting.

If you can do it in under one minute you are a fast and fluent winner!

But if you are not happy with your result – just try once more.

▶ Spot the keys

You practised listening for key words when you asked the way to the post office in Week 3. Now you are in a department store. You have asked the sales assistant if the black shoes you liked are also available in size 44 (Italian).

She said **no** then **un momento, per favore** and disappeared. When she came back this is what she said:

> *Ho appena guardato in magazzino se ne rimaneva* **una nella sua taglia, ma c'è solo in verde. Ma questo** *modello è tagliato piuttosto* **grande**, *quindi* **credo che la taglia quarantadue** *possa* **andare bene per Lei**.

It appears that size 44 was only available in green but she felt that size 42 might be big enough.

Test your progress

1 Did you say that somebody has telephoned? Signor Gucci?
2 I would like to know where the restaurants are.
3 It is late and he is not there. What are we doing tonight?
4 Here is the menu! Do you know the wines of (the) Tuscany?
5 The cash dispenser is upstairs, behind the exit, near the door.
6 Wednesday we must go to the doctor. It is an important appointment.
7 Why do you say she is boring? Because I know her well.
8 Have you seen him? I must go to Pisa with him.
9 (The) Signor Rossini is my client. He has bought everything.
10 I would like to buy this thing. How does one say in Italian…?
11 Next week? I am sorry. It is not possible.
12 There is too much. Please help me. Many thanks!
13 Eighty euros for two days? Very interesting. Yes, of course we take it.
14 I must buy three things for my friends.
15 He says that he has a (the) cold and that he has not finished his work.
16 Can they eat only the minestrone?
17 Please help me. There is a terrible dog.
18 Nobody has seen who has eaten the steak.
19 Can I say something: the chicken is not bad, but the fish is better.
20 What do you take? The fruit? Yes, sure, it is from (the) Tuscany.

How are your 'shares' looking on the **Progress chart**? Going up?

05

week five

How about 15 minutes on the train, tube or bus, 10 minutes on the way home and 20 minutes before switching on the television...?

Day one

- Read **On the move**.
- Listen to/Read **In viaggio**.
- Read the **New words**. Learn 15 or more.

Day two

- Repeat **In viaggio** and the **New words**.
- Cut out the **Flash words** and get stuck in.

Day three

- Test yourself to perfection on all the **New words**.
- Listen to/Read **Learn by heart**.

Day four

- Read and learn the **Good news grammar**.
- Cut out and learn the **Flash sentences**.

Day five

- Listen to/Read **Let's speak Italian**.
- Listen to/Read **Spot the keys**.

Day six

- Listen to/Read **Let's speak more Italian** (optional).
- Listen to/Read **Let's speak Italian – fast and fluently** (optional).
- Translate **Test your progress**.

Day seven

How is the Progress chart looking? Great?... Great!
I bet you don't want a day off... but I insist!

day-by-day guide

On the move

Tom and Kate are travelling through the lakes of Northern Italy – by train, bus and hire car. They talk to Nina, the ticket clerk at the station, to Jim on the train and later to Mario, the bus driver.

(At the station)

Tom	Two tickets for Como, please.
Nina	Thereandback?
Tom	There and what? Can you speak more slowly please?
Nina	There – and – back?
Tom	No, one way only. At what time is there a train and from which platform?
Nina	At 9.56. Platform eight.
Kate	Quickly Tom, here are two seats, non-smoking. Oh, but someone is smoking. Excuse me, you (one) cannot smoke, because it is non-smoking here. It is forbidden to smoke.
Jim	I am sorry. I don't understand. I speak only English.

(At the bus stop)

Kate	There is no bus. We have to wait 20 minutes. Tom, here are my postcards. Over there is a letterbox. I would like to take some photos. The lake is beautiful with the sun.
Tom	Kate, quickly! There are a lot of people. Here are two buses! Both are blue. This one is full. Let's take the other one. *(On the bus)* Two for Milan, please.
Mario	This bus goes only to Como.
Tom	But we are in Como!
Mario	Yes, yes, but this is the bus for the hospital of Como.

(In the car)

Tom	Here is our car. Only €40 for three days. I am very pleased.
Kate	I do not like the car. It costs so little because it is very old. Let's hope that we don't have problems.
Tom	I am sorry. The first car was too expensive and the second (one) too big. This was the last one.
	(Later) Where are we? The map has disappeared! On the left there is a petrol station, and on the right there is a school. Come on, quickly!

⸺▶ Page 66

▶ In viaggio

Tom and Kate are travelling through the lakes of Northern Italy – by train, bus and hire car. They talk to Nina, the ticket clerk at the station, to Jim on the train and later to Mario, the bus driver.

(Alla stazione)

Tom	Due biglietti per Como, per favore.
Nina	Andataeritorno?
Tom	Andata e cosa? Può parlare più lentamente per favore.
Nina	Andata – e – ritorno?
Tom	No, solo andata. A che ora c'è un treno e da che binario?
Nina	Alle nove e cinquantasei. Binario otto.
Kate	Presto Tom, qui ci sono due posti 'non fumatori'. Oh, ma qualcuno fuma. Scusi, non si può fumare, perché qui è 'non fumatori'. È proibito fumare.
Jim	I am sorry. Non capisco. Parlo only English.

(Alla fermata dell'autobus)

Kate	Non c'è l'autobus. Dobbiamo aspettare venti minuti. Tom, ecco le mie cartoline. Là c'è una buca delle lettere. Vorrei fare delle foto. Il lago è bellissimo con il sole!
Tom	Kate, presto! C'è molta gente. Ecco due autobus! Tutti e due sono blu. Questo è pieno. Prendiamo l'altro. *(Nel autobus)* Due per Milano per favore.
Mario	Quest'autobus va solo fino a Como.
Tom	Ma siamo a Como!
Mario	Sì, sì, ma questo è l'autobus per l'ospedale di Como.

(In auto)

Tom	Ecco la nostra auto. Solo quaranta euro per tre giorni. Sono molto contento.
Kate	L'auto non mi piace. Costa così poco perché è molto vecchia. Speriamo di non avere problemi.
Tom	Mi dispiace. La prima auto era troppo cara e la seconda troppo grande. Questa era l'ultima.
	(Più tardi) Dove siamo? La cartina è sparita! A sinistra c'è un benzinaio, e a destra c'è una scuola. Dai, presto!

⋯⟶ Page 67

Kate We are coming from the underground station. The main road is at the traffic light. It's perhaps three kilometres to the motorway. *(On the motorway)* Why does the car go so slowly? Have we enough petrol? How many litres? Do we have oil? Is the engine not too hot? They have given us a broken car. Where is the mobile phone? Where is the number of the mechanic (garage)? Where is my bag?

Tom Kate, **please**! All this gives me a headache. And now comes also the rain! And why are the police behind us?

▶ New words

in viaggio *on the move, travelling*
la stazione (railway) *station*
biglietto *ticket*
andata e ritorno *return ticket* ('going and returning')
parlare *to speak*
più *more*
lentamente *slowly*
treno *train*
binario *track, platform*
presto *quick, quickly*
non fumatori *non-smoking*
fuma *he/she/it smokes, you smoke*
si può/non si può *one can/ one cannot*
fumare *to smoke*
proibito *forbidden*
non capisco *I don't understand*
parlo *I speak*
fermata *stop*
aspettare *to wait*
cartolina *postcard*
buca delle lettere *letter box*
la foto, le foto *the photo, the photos*
lago *lake*
bellissimo/a *very beautiful*

il sole *the sun*
la gente *the people*
tutti e due *both* ('all and two')
pieno/a *full*
altro/a *other*
l'ospedale *the hospital*
l'auto (la) *the car*
giorno, giorni *day, days*
contento/a *pleased, happy*
mi piace/non mi piace *I like/ I do not like*
così *so*
vecchio/a *old*
speriamo *we hope, let's hope*
i problemi *the problems*
primo/a *first*
secondo/a *second*
ultimo/a *last*
cartina *map*
sparito/a *disappeared*
benzinaio *petrol station*
dai! *come on!*
veniamo *we come, we are coming*
strada principale *main road*
semaforo *traffic light*
chilometro *kilometre*
autostrada *motorway*
benzina *petrol*
litro, litri *litre, litres*

Kate   Veniamo dalla fermata del metro. La strada principale è al semaforo. Sono forse tre chilometri fino all'autostrada. *(In autostrada)* Perché l'auto va così lentamente? Abbiamo abbastanza benzina? Quanti litri? Abbiamo olio? Il motore non è troppo caldo? Ci hanno dato un'auto rotta. Dov'è il telefonino? Dov'è il numero del meccanico? Dov'è la mia borsa?

Tom   Kate, **per favore!** Tutto questo mi fa venire il mal di testa! E adesso viene anche la pioggia! E perché c'è la polizia dietro di noi?

il motore	*the motor, engine*	**fa**	*he/she/it makes, you make*
caldo/a	*hot*	**venire**	*to come*
ci	*us*	**il mal di testa**	*the headache*
dare/dato	*give/given*	**pioggia**	*rain*
meccanico	*mechanic (at a garage)*	**polizia**	*police*
		noi	*us, we*

TOTAL NEW WORDS: 63
...only 31 words to go!

▶ Learn by heart

Someone has crashed the car and someone else is getting suspicious...! Try to say these lines fluently and like a prize-winning play!

Andiamo al tennis

A   Andiamo al tennis. Mi piacciono i due americani.
Ho dei biglietti della mia ditta.
Prendiamo l'autobus, o meglio, il metro.
C'è anche un treno tutto il giorno.

B   L'autobus? Il metro? Un treno?
Perché? Cosa c'è?
Abbiamo un'auto laggiù*.

A   Beh... ieri, con la pioggia, non ho visto il semaforo.
Però è poco, solo la porta, e il meccanico era molto simpatico!

*****laggiù:** *down there*

▶ Good news grammar

1 Confusing: *mi, me, Lei, gli, ci, noi, la, lo, lui, lei*

You have come across these little words in the stories and the **New words**. Some appeared before the verbs: <u>ci</u> hanno dato, *they have given us*. And some were stuck onto the end: Posso aiutar<u>la</u>? *Can I help you?* or Può far<u>lo</u>, *Can you do it?* Feel like pulling out your hair?

Learning these little words 'cold' is quite difficult, but when they come up in the **Flash sentences** or the texts, it's not so bad. And when you speak **Instant Italian** you can muddle them up or avoid them altogether. No problem.

I have extracted six easy and useful ones. Spend five minutes learning them and take another five minutes to remember them.

for me	per **me**	*for her*	per **lei**
for you	per **Lei**	*for us*	per **noi**
for him	per **lui**	*for them*	per **loro**

You use the same words with **con, a** and **da.**
> **con me**: *with me*, **a Lei**: *to you*, **da loro**: *from them*, or *at their house.*

2 *Mi piace – non mi piace*

You will use this all the time. Think how often you use *I like – I don't like* in English!

You can like or not like *things* or *doing things*:

> **Mi piace** la sua scuola. **Mi piace** mangiare con lui. **Non mi piace** il pesce. **Mi piace** molto!

If you like more than one thing, you say **mi piacciono**: mi piacciono i negozi; **non mi piacciono** i ristoranti.

3 A reminder: *ho bisogno*

Remember **ho bisogno** from Week 1?

> **Ho bisogno di** molti soldi. It literally means *I have need of…* . This is just a reminder to use it.
> **Ho bisogno di** un medico.
> **Abbiamo bisogno di** un meccanico… Anche noi!

▶ Let's speak Italian

A ten-point warm-up: I give you an answer and you ask me a question as if you did not hear the words in CAPITAL LETTERS very well.

Example Lucia è ALLA POSTA.
Ask Dov'è Lucia?

1 Il telefonino è NELLA MIA BORSA.
2 Sono stato/a in ospedale IN MARZO.
3 Tom vorrebbe parlare CON MARCELLO.
4 Per Pisa, andata e ritorno costa €15.
5 Non ho visto IL SEMAFORO.
6 SÌ, sono contento della scuola.
7 NO, la cartina non mi piace.
8 Vanno in Inghilterra CON LA FERRARI.
9 La casa non mi piace PERCHÉ È MOLTO VECCHIA.
10 Le vacanze erano BELLISSIME.

Answer in Italian using 'yes' or 'no'. Speak about yourself.

11 Ha visto il benzinaio?
12 Prende questo treno?
13 Va adesso alla stazione?
14 Le piace il lago?
15 Può fumare qui?

Explain these words in Italian. Your answers can differ from mine.

16 an au pair   19 unemployed
17 kennels   20 to be broke
18 teacher

Answers

1 Dov'è il telefonino?
2 Quando è stato/a in ospedale?
3 Con chi vorrebbe parlare Tom?
4 Quanto costa per Pisa, andata e ritorno?
5 Cosa non ha visto?
6 È contento della scuola?
7 Le piace la cartina?
8 Come vanno in Inghilterra?
9 Perché non le piace la casa?
10 Com'erano le vacanze?
11 Sì, l'ho visto./ No, non l'ho visto.
12 Sì, lo prendo. No, non lo prendo.
13 Sì, vado adesso. No, non vado adesso.
14 Sì, mi piace. No, non mi piace.
15 Sì, qui posso fumare. No, qui non posso fumare.
16 Una signora che aiuta in casa con tutto il lavoro.
17 Una casa per il cane quando siamo in vacanza.
18 Qualcuno che lavora nella scuola con i bambini.
19 Qualcuno che non ha lavoro.
20 Non abbiamo più soldi. Sono finiti.

▶ Let's speak more Italian

In your own words

This exercise will teach you to express yourself freely. Use only the words you have learned so far.

Tell me in your own words that ...

1 you bought a return ticket to Como
2 there is a train at 10.15 from platform eight
3 it is forbidden, but somebody is smoking in a non-smoking seat
4 on Monday you would like to go to Milan by bus
5 you must take some photos for your mother
6 this bus is 'chock-a-block'; you (pl.) are going to take the other one
7 the car is cheap because it is very old
8 your wife says: 'They have given us a broken car'
9 the car goes so slowly and the engine overheats
10 hopefully you won't have problems

Answers

1 Ho comprato un biglietto di andata e ritorno per Como.
2 C'è un treno alle dieci e un quarto dal binario otto.
3 È proibito, ma qualcuno fuma in un posto 'non fumatori'.
4 Lunedì vorrei andare a Milano in autobus.
5 Devo fare delle foto per mia madre.
6 Questo autobus è pieno. Prendiamo l'altro.
7 L'auto costa poco perché è molto vecchia.
8 Mia moglie dice: 'Ci hanno dato un'auto rotta.'
9 L'auto va così lentamente e il motore è troppo caldo.
10 Speriamo di non avere problemi.

Translate each section and check if it is correct, then cover up the answers and say the three or four sentences fast!

25 seconds per section for a silver star, 20 seconds for a gold star.

Some of the English is in 'Italian-speak' to help you.

A ticket to Milan, please, only one way.
How much? €21? Can you speak more slowly, please?
Thank you. When does the train leave?

Un biglietto per Milano, per favore, solo andata.
Quanto? Ventun euro? Può parlare più lentamente, per favore?
Grazie. A che ora parte il treno?

We would like to take the bus.
We have to wait twenty minutes.
We can take a photo of the lake.

Vorremmo prendere l'autobus.
Dobbiamo aspettare venti minuti.
Possiamo fare una foto del lago.

We don't have (a) map of Italy.
It's ten kilometres to the motorway.
The traffic light is red.
We have a problem. Perhaps our car is broken.
My wife has a headache.

Non abbiamo una cartina dell'Italia.
Sono dieci chilometri fino all'autostrada.
Il semaforo è rosso.
Abbiamo un problema. Forse la nostra auto è rotta.
Mia moglie ha mal di testa.

Now say **all** the sentences in Italian without stopping and starting.

If you can do it in under one minute you are a fast and fluent winner!

But if you are not happy with your result – just try once more.

▶ Spot the keys

This time you plan a trip in the country and wonder about the weather.

You   **Scusi, vorrei sapere che tempo fa.**

Answer   **Non so cosa** *dicano le previsioni* **in televisione** *ma mi sembra di avere capito che c'è una perturbazione che arriva. Farà ancora piuttosto* **caldo, più o meno venticinque** *gradi, ma prima di* **stasera** *avremo sicuramente della* **pioggia**.

He doesn't know something on television (?) but you heard the word **hot** and then **more or less 25** (degrees centigrade). You also understood **this evening** and **rain**. Perhaps you'd better take an umbrella!

Test your progress

1   It is forbidden to go to the restaurant without shoes.
2   I like your Lamborghini. Was it very cheap?
3   When I am travelling (on the move) I always speak a lot of Italian.
4   I need six tickets. Are there non-smoking seats?
5   Let's hope we don't have (not to have) problems with the engine.
6   I do not like the Internet. It is difficult. I believe I am (to be) too old.
7   I do not understand. Can you speak more slowly, please?
8   It is hot and there are a lot of people here. Let's go to the lake.
9   One hour with her gives me (me makes come) a (the) headache.
10 There is a bus at the traffic lights. Where is it going?
11 The credit card has (is) disappeared. We have to telephone the police.
12 Let's do it like this: first we buy the Ferrari for me and afterwards a T-shirt for you.
13 I like this car, but the other (one) was better.
14 We have only a litre of petrol and there is not a petrol station until Naples.
15 I like the sun and I like the rain. I like both.
16 *(On the phone)* Hello, we are 20 km from Pisa. Is there a mechanic?
17 Excuse me, can you help me, please? I do not know Rome. Where is the station?
18 The main street? It is not difficult if you take the metro.
19 Where are they? What have they done? I do not like to wait.
20 We are coming from (the) platform 17. Where is Mario?

06

week six

This is your last week! Need I say more?

Day one

- Read **In the airport**.
- Listen to/Read **In aeroporto**.
- Read the **New words**. There are only 31!

Day two

- Repeat **In aeroporto** and learn all the **New words**.
- Work with the **Flash words** and **Flash sentences**.

Day three

- Test yourself on the **Flash sentences**.
- No more **Good news grammar!** Have a look at the summary.

Day four

- Listen to/Read and learn **Arrivederci!**
- Read **Say it simply**.

Day five

- Listen to/Read **Spot the keys**.
- Listen to/Read **Let's speak Italian**.

Day six

- Listen to/Read **Let's speak more Italian** (optional).
- Listen to/Read **Let's speak Italian – fast and fluently** (optional).
- Your last **Test your progress!** Go for it!

Day seven

Congratulations!

You have successfully completed the course and can now speak

Instant Italian!

In the airport

Tom and Kate are on their way home to Birmingham. They are in the departure lounge of Milan airport.

Tom   On Monday we must work. Terrible! I would rather go to Miami or Honolulu. Nobody knows where I am and the office can wait.

Kate   And **my** company? What do they do? They speak with my mother! She has the number of my mobile. And then?

Tom   Yes, yes, I know (it). Well, perhaps at Christmas we'll go for a week in the snow or to Madeira on a ship... There is a kiosk down there. I'll go and buy a newspaper... Kate! There is Gino Pavarotti!

Gino   Hello. How are you? What are you doing here? This is my wife, Nancy. Are the holidays over? How were they?

Kate   Italy is wonderful. We have seen a lot and eaten too much. Now we know Tuscany and the lakes very well.

Gino   Next year Venice! What a fantastic city!... Mrs Walker, my wife would like to buy a book about computers. Can you go with her and help her, please? Mr Walker, you have the newspaper. Are there any photos of the football? And then are we going to drink something?

(At the kiosk)

Kate   There is nothing here. I do not see anything of interest. Are you also going to England?

Nancy   No, we are going to Pisa to Gino's mother. Our children are often with her during the holidays. Tomorrow we'll take the train. It costs less.

Kate   Your husband works at the Bank of Italy?

Nancy   Yes. The work is interesting, but the money is little. We have an apartment (which is) too small for us and an old car. It always needs a lot of repairs. My family lives in California and my girlfriend is in Florida and we write a lot of e-mails. I would like to go to America but it is too expensive.

Kate   But you have a beautiful house in Portofino.

Nancy   A house in Portofino? I have never been to Portofino. When we have holidays we go to a friend in Genoa.

······➡ Page 78

▶ In aeroporto

Tom and Kate are on their way home to Birmingham. They are in the departure lounge of Milan airport.

Tom   Lunedì dobbiamo lavorare. Terribile! Vorrei invece andare a Miami o a Honolulu. Nessuno sa dove sono e la ditta può aspettare.

Kate   E la **mia** ditta? Cosa fanno? Parlano con mia madre! Lei ha il numero del mio telefonino. E poi…?

Tom   Sì, sì, lo so. Allora, forse a Natale andiamo una settimana sulla neve o a Madeira in nave… C'è un chiosco laggiù. Vado a comprare un giornale… Kate! C'è Gino Pavarotti!

Gino   Salve! Come va? Cosa fa qui? Questa è mia moglie, Nancy. Sono finite le vacanze? Come sono state?

Kate   L'Italia è meravigliosa. Abbiamo visto molto e mangiato troppo. Adesso conosciamo la Toscana e i laghi molto bene.

Gino   Il prossimo anno Venezia! Che città fantastica!… Signora Walker, mia moglie vorrebbe comprare un libro di computer. Per favore, può andare con lei e aiutarla? Signor Walker, Lei ha il giornale. Ci sono delle foto del calcio? E poi andiamo a bere qualcosa?

(Al chiosco)

Kate   Qui non c'è niente. Non vedo niente di interessante. Va anche Lei in Inghilterra?

Nancy   No, andiamo a Pisa dalla madre di Gino. I nostri bambini sono spesso da lei durante le vacanze. Domani prendiamo il treno. Costa meno.

Kate   Suo marito lavora alla Banca d'Italia?

Nancy   Sì. Il lavoro è interessante, ma i soldi sono pochi. Abbiamo un appartamento troppo piccolo per noi e una vecchia auto. Ha bisogno sempre di molte riparazioni. La mia famiglia vive in California e la mia amica è in Florida e ci scriviamo molte e-mail. Vorrei andare in America ma costa troppo.

Kate   Ma Lei ha una bella casa a Portofino.

Nancy   Una casa a Portofino? Non sono mai stata a Portofino. Quando abbiamo le vacanze andiamo a Genova da un amico.

⋯⟹ Page 79

Tom	Kate, come on, quickly. We must go. Goodbye! What is the matter, Kate? What did Mrs Pavarotti say?
Kate	Wait, Tom, wait..:!

▶ New words

aeroporto *airport*
invece (di) *instead (of), on the other hand*
la madre *the mother*
sa *he/she/it knows, you know*
fanno *they do, make*
parlano *they speak*
lo so *I know it*
Natale *Christmas*
la neve *the snow*
la nave *the ship*
chiosco *kiosk*
laggiù *down there*
salve *hello (not quite as familiar as ciao)*
come va? *how are you?*
meraviglioso/a *wonderful*
conosciamo *we know*

città *town, city*
fantastico/a *fantastic*
vorrebbe *he/she/it/you would like*
libro *book*
vedo *I see*
durante *during*
spesso *often*
appartamento *apartment, flat*
le riparazioni *the repairs*
famiglia *family*
vive *he/she/it lives, you live*
scriviamo *we write*
mai *never, ever*
che cosa c'è? *what's the matter?*
aspetta! *wait!*

TOTAL NEW WORDS: 31
TOTAL ITALIAN WORDS LEARNED: 379
EXTRA WORDS: 79

GRAND TOTAL: 458

| Tom | Kate, dai, presto. Dobbiamo andare. Arrivederci! Che cosa c'è, Kate? Cosa ha detto la Signora Pavarotti? |
| Kate | Aspetta, Tom, aspetta...! |

▶ Learn by heart

This is your last dialogue to learn by heart. Give it your best!
You now have six prize-winning party pieces, and a large store
of everyday sayings which will be very useful.

Arrivederci...!

| Kate | Pronto. Buongiorno Signor Verdi. Sono Kate Walker. Siamo all'aeroporto. Sì, le vacanze sono finite. Che bella, l'Italia! Tom vorrebbe parlare con Lei. Un momento per favore e... arrivederci! |
| Tom | Ciao, Bruno! Cosa? Ha comprato tutti e due? C'è un e-mail della ditta? Benissimo! Mille grazie! L'anno prossimo? Kate vorrebbe andare a Capri, ma io vorrei vedere* Venezia. Con Edith Palmer? **Per favore!** Dobbiamo andare. Dunque... a presto! Ciao! Arrivederci! |

*vedere: (to) see

Good news grammar

As promised there is no new grammar in this lesson, just a summary of all the **Instant** verbs which appear in the six weeks. The 31 verbs are not for learning, just for a quick check. You know and have used most of them!

Basic form	I	you, he, she, it	we	they	Past
avere	ho	ha	abbiamo	hanno	avuto
aiutare	aiuto	aiuta	aiutiamo	aiutano	aiutato
andare	vado	va	andiamo	vanno	(sono) andato
aspettare	aspetto	aspetta	aspettiamo	aspettano	aspettato
bere	bevo	beve	beviamo	bevono	bevuto
capire	capisco	capisce	capiamo	capiscono	capito
comprare	compro	compra	compriamo	comprano	comprato
conoscere	conosco	conosce	conosciamo	conoscono	conosciuto
costare		costa		costano	
credere	credo	crede	crediamo	credono	creduto
dare	do	dà	diamo	danno	dato
desiderare	desidero	desidera	desideriamo	desiderano	desiderato
dire	dico	dice	diciamo	dicono	detto
dovere	devo	deve	dobbiamo	devono	dovuto
essere	sono	è	siamo	sono	(sono) stato
(imperf.)	era	era	eravamo	erano	
fare	faccio	fa	facciamo	fanno	fatto
fumare	fumo	fuma	fumiamo	fumano	fumato
lavorare	lavoro	lavora	lavoriamo	lavorano	lavorato
mangiare	mangio	mangia	mangiamo	mangiano	mangiato
parlare	parlo	parla	parliamo	parlano	parlato
passare	passo	passa	passiamo	passano	passato
potere	posso	può	possiamo	possono	potuto
prendere	prendo	prende	prendiamo	prendono	preso
riparare	riparo	ripara	ripariamo	riparano	riparato
sapere	so	sa	sappiamo	sanno	saputo
scrivere	scrivo	scrive	scriviamo	scrivono	scritto
sperare	spero	spera	speriamo	sperano	sperato
telefonare	telefono	telefona	telefoniamo	telefonano	telefonato
vedere	vedo	vede	vediamo	vedono	visto
venire	vengo	viene	veniamo	vengono	sono venuto
(volere)	vorrei	vorrebbe	vorremmo	vorrebbero	

Say it simply

1 Imagine you are at the dry cleaner's. You want to know if the item you have brought to be cleaned can be done by the end of the day since you are leaving for Verona early tomorrow morning. You also want to explain that the stain may be red wine.

Think of what you could say in simple Italian, using the words you know. Then write it down and compare it with my suggestion on page 90.

2 You are at the airport, about to catch your flight home when you realize that you have left some clothes behind in the room of your hotel. You phone the hotel to ask the housekeeper to send the things on to you.

What would you say? Formulate your telephone call and say it. Then write it down and compare it with the one on page 90.

▶ Spot the keys

Here are two final practice rounds. If you have the recording, close the book now.

1 This time, the key words are not shown. When you have found them see if you can get the gist of it. My answer is on page 90.

This is what you might ask of a taxi driver:

A quanti minuti è l'aeroporto e quanto costa?

And this could be the reply:

Dipende da quando va. Normalmente ci vogliono venti minuti, ma se c'è traffico e se c'è la coda sul ponte ci metterà almeno trentacinque minuti. Il prezzo lo può vedere sul tachimetro. Più o meno saranno dai venti ai venticinque euro.

2 While in the departure lounge of the airport, you overheard someone raving about something. Identify the key words and guess where they have been. The answer is on page 90.

...e anche mio marito dice che delle vacanze così gli piacciono moltissimo, molto di più di quelle dello scorso anno. La gente era proprio simpatica e molto più amabile che da noi. L'hotel era situato proprio in riva al lago; abbiamo fatto delle belle camminate e il tempo è stato bellissimo. Abbiamo mangiato benissimo e il prossimo anno ci ritorneremo certamente in...

▶ Let's speak Italian

Here's a five-point warm-up: answer these questions using the words in brackets.

1 Ha comprato l'appartamento? (sì, lo)
2 Sa che fanno a Natale? (sì, niente)
3 Quando ha visto suo marito? (ieri)
4 Perché va in Inghilterra? (famiglia, vive, là)
5 Com'è l'Italia? (meravigliosa)

In your last exercise you are going to interpret again, this time telling your Italian friend what others have said in English. Each time say the whole sentence OUT LOUD, translating the English words in brackets.

6 Il mio amico ha detto che... (*the holidays are finished*).
7 Ha detto anche che... (*we are going to Venice next year*).
8 Mia moglie vorrebbe sapere... (*when you go to Los Angeles*).
9 Vorrebbe anche sapere... (*what they said*).
10 Mio marito dice che... (*he cannot come*).
11 Angela non può venire perché... (*she works on a ship*).
12 Il mio amico dice che... (*you are very nice*).
13 Dice anche che... (*he would like to have your phone number*).
14 C'è qualcuno che vorrebbe sapere... (*what you did*).
15 Mia madre dice che... (*she likes the shops*).
16 Nessuno sa... (*where he has been in America*).
17 I miei amici non sanno... (*who took the car*).
18 Qualcuno sa... (*how one can get to Lago Maggiore*).
19 Non so... (*how much the repairs cost*).
20 Kate Walker sa... (*where you can buy **Instant Italian***).

Answers

1 Sì, l'ho comprato.
2 Sì, non fanno niente.
3 L'ho visto ieri.
4 Perché la mia famiglia vive là.
5 L'Italia è meravigliosa.
6 ...le vacanze sono finite.
7 ...andiamo a Venezia l'anno prossimo.
8 ...quando va a Los Angeles.
9 ...cosa hanno detto.
10 ...non può venire.
11 ...lavora su una nave.
12 ...Lei è molto simpatico/a.
13 ...vorrebbe avere il suo numero di telefono.
14 ...cosa ha fatto.
15 ...le piacciono i negozi.
16 ...dov'è stato in America.
17 ...chi ha preso l'auto.
18 ...come si può andare al Lago Maggiore.
19 ...quanto costano le riparazioni.
20 ...dove si può comprare **Instant Italian**.

▶ Let's speak more Italian

In your own words

This exercise will teach you to express yourself freely. Use only the words you have learned so far.

Tell me in your own words that...

1 next week you have to work
2 you don't like to work; you'd rather have more holidays
3 nobody knows that you are in Milan
4 your mother has the number of your mobile phone
5 your vacation in Tuscany (Toscana) was wonderful
6 you did a lot of sightseeing and ate too much
7 your friend Pavarotti works for the Bank of Italy
8 he is going to catch a train to Pisa tomorrow
9 your wife must go to California because her father is ill
10 you would like to go to Miami for Christmas, but by boat

Answers

1 La settimana prossima devo lavorare.
2 Non mi piace lavorare. Vorrei fare più vacanze.
3 Nessuno sa che sono a Milano.
4 Mia madre ha il numero del mio telefonino.
5 La mia vacanza in Toscana era meravigliosa.
6 Ho visto molto e ho mangiato troppo.
7 Il mio amico Pavarotti lavora alla Banca d'Italia.
8 Prende il treno per Pisa domani.
9 Mia moglie deve andare in California perché suo padre è malato.
10 Vorrei andare a Miami a Natale, ma in nave.

▶ Let's speak Italian – fast and fluently

Translate each section and check if it is correct, then cover up the answers and say the three or four sentences fast!

30 seconds for a silver star, 20 seconds for a gold star.

My company can wait.
Nobody knows where I am.
We call my mother on the mobile.

La mia ditta può aspettare.
Nessuno sa dove sono.
Chiamiamo mia madre sul telefonino.

Next year she would like to go to Venice.
Would you like to come with me?
I don't see anything of interest.

L'anno prossimo lei vorrebbe andare a Venezia.
Vorrebbe venire con me?
Non vedo niente di interessante.

Hello, what are you doing here? What's the matter?
I need to repair my car and my flat. They are very old.
Can you help me, please – with 200 euros?

Salve, cosa fa qui? Che cosa c'è?
Devo riparare l'auto e l'appartamento. Sono molto vecchi.
Può aiutarmi, per favore – con duecento euro?

Now say **all** the sentences in Italian without stopping and starting.

If you can do it in under one minute you are a fast and fluent winner!

But if you are not happy with your result – just try once more.

Test your progress

Thirty **Instant** verbs have been crammed into this text! But don't panic – it looks worse than it is. Go for it – you'll do brilliantly!

Translate into Italian:

1 We write many e-mails because we have a new computer.
2 Hello, can I help? Your bag has gone? Where can it be?
3 Who knows the number of his mobile phone? I am sorry, I don't know it.
4 How are you? I am pleased that you do not smoke (any) more.
5 Would you like to see Bologna? It is a big town.
6 I do not like January. There is snow and it is often very cold.
7 There is a kiosk down there. Would you like something to drink?
8 Why have they not phoned? We waited until yesterday.
9 I'll take the book. He says that it is interesting.
10 I believe that the airport is always open, day and night.
11 It is important to know how much the client has bought.
12 Have you seen the English newspaper? I do not like the photo. It is ugly.
13 He said that he has (the) cold. He hopes to come tomorrow.
14 Is an apartment near the centre expensive in Italy?
15 We both have to work. Three boys and two girls cost a lot.
16 I am going at Christmas. I prefer December for my holidays instead of July.
17 We know Marcello very well. Do you like him?
18 Can you give me the dog? He is small but nice. What does he eat?
19 Her mother is here. She does not speak Italian.
20 Don't you know it? The repairs costs 500 euros.
21 I must go to the cash dispenser. I need money.
22 I am sorry but **Instant Italian** is now finished.

Check your answers on page 89. Now go to the **Progress chart** and work out your final score for the course. You'll be proud of yourself!

answers

How to score

From a total of 100%
- Subtract 1% for each wrong or missing word.
- Subtract 1% for the wrong form of the verb. Example *we have* ho (abbiamo).
- Subtract 1% every time you mix up the present and the past tenses.

There are no penalties for:
- wrong use of all those little words, like: **il, la, un, una, il suo, la sua, da il (dal), in il (nel)**, etc.
- wrong ending of adjectives, e.g. **un'amica americano.**
- wrong choice of words with similar meaning, e.g.: **a, in, da.**
- wrong or different word order.
- wrong spelling/missing accents/missing apostrophes – as long as you can *say* the word, e.g.: **bisonyo (bisogno); com'e, comè (com'è).**

**100% LESS YOUR PENALTIES WILL GIVE YOU
YOUR WEEKLY SCORE**

Week 1: Test your progress
1 Buongiorno, siamo Helen e Jane.
2 Sono di Roma, anche Lei?
3 Dove lavora adesso?
4 Sono stato/stata a Milano in ottobre.
5 La mia amica è in Italia per un anno.
6 Andiamo sempre a Pisa in giugno.
7 Ho lavorato alla Fiat in maggio.
8 Che cosa/cosa fa a Londra?
9 Lavoro in una scuola ma senza soldi.
10 La casa grande a Bologna è per i bambini.

11 Un momento, per favore, dov'è Luigi?
12 La casa ha il telefono? No, purtroppo.
13 Costa molto la Ferrari? Sì, certo, costa troppo.
14 Com'è il lavoro in Italia? Buono?
15 Mario ha un amico/un'amica in una ditta americana.
16 Siamo stati/state a Como per tre giorni.
17 Abbiamo i posti buoni in aereo.
18 Ho sempre le vacanze noiose.
19 Ho bisogno di una bella moglie, una Lamborghini e molti soldi...
20 Telefona adesso con una ditta a Londra.

Correct your answers.
YOUR SCORE: _____ %   Then read them out loud twice.

Week 2: Test your progress

1 Dove c'è un telefono?
2 Scusi, abbiamo solo la carta di credito.
3 Possiamo mangiare alle sette domani?
4 Ha una tavola abbastanza grande? Siamo in cinque.
5 Le camere piccole non hanno il bagno.
6 Vorremmo mangiare prosciutto e melone.
7 Possiamo andare dalle sei alle sette meno un quarto.
8 Dove possiamo bere qualcosa?
9 Siamo stati al bar dalle nove alle dieci e mezza.
10 Va bene, prendiamo la Fiat per un giorno.
11 Quanto costa la prima colazione? Solo cinque euro.
12 Andiamo a riparare il computer. È rotto.
13 Com'è il latte? Il bambino lo può bere?
14 Dove sono i servizi, a destra o a sinistra?
15 Posso andare a Hollywood – senza mio marito?
16 Un caffè per favore – niente per Lei?
17 Dov'è la Signora Rossi? Forse nel bar?
18 Tre euro e dieci per un tè freddo – è un po' caro...!
19 Sono stato in Toscana in febbraio. Non è male.
20 Ci sono trecento bar qui, uno a cento metri da qui.

YOUR SCORE: ___ %

Week 3: Test your progress

1 Prima, vorrei passare al Bankomat.
2 In questo negozio le scarpe costano troppo.
3 Ha visto mio marito in farmacia?
4 Siamo stati qui fino alle dieci e un quarto.

5 Abbiamo visto il tennis in Inghilterra, in televisione.
6 Mi dispiace, non abbiamo lo stesso in rosso, nella taglia 44.
7 Questo negozio non è conveniente.
8 Chi ha riparato il mio telefono? Lei?
9 Ecco il grande magazzino. Però non è aperto!
10 Oggi non abbiamo comprato troppo, solo pane e mezzo chilo di burro.
11 Ho mangiato tutto – uova, mele, patate e un pezzo di formaggio.
12 Dobbiamo fare spese. È questo il centro?
13 Ieri sono stato/stata in ditta fino alle nove.
14 I giornali inglesi costano molto in Italia.
15 C'è un autobus? No? Non importa.
16 Era un commesso molto simpatico.
17 Cos'è questo? Qualcosa per noi?
18 Ha comprato la borsa qui vicino o alla UPIM?
19 Era tutto molto caro. Dunque non ho comprato niente.
20 Abbiamo bisogno di tre chili, credo.

YOUR SCORE: ___ %

Week 4: Test your progress

1 Ha detto che qualcuno ha telefonato? Il Signor Gucci?
2 Vorrei sapere dove sono i ristoranti.
3 È tardi e non c'è. Cosa facciamo stasera?
4 Ecco il menù! Conosce i vini della Toscana?
5 Il Bankomat è su, dietro all'uscita, vicino alla porta.
6 Mercoledì dobbiamo andare dal medico. È un appuntamento importante.
7 Perché dice che è noiosa? Perché la conosco bene.
8 Lo ha visto? Devo andare a Pisa con lui.
9 Il Signor Rossini è il mio cliente. Ha comprato tutto.
10 Vorrei comprare questa cosa. Come si dice in italiano…?
11 La settimana prossima? Mi dispiace. Non è possibile.
12 C'è troppo. Mi aiuti per favore. Grazie mille!
13 Ottanta euro per due giorni? Molto interessante. Sì, naturalmente lo/la prendiamo.
14 Devo comprare tre cose per i miei amici.
15 Dice che ha il raffreddore e che non ha finito il suo lavoro.
16 Possono mangiare solo il minestrone?
17 Mi aiuti per favore. C'è un cane terribile.
18 Nessuno ha visto chi ha mangiato la bistecca.
19 Posso dire qualcosa: il pollo non è male ma il pesce è meglio.
20 Cosa prende? La frutta? Sì certo, è della Toscana.

YOUR SCORE: ___ %

Week 5: Test your progress

1 È proibito andare al ristorante senza scarpe.
2 Mi piace la sua Lamborghini. Era molto conveniente?
3 Quando sono in viaggio parlo sempre molto italiano.
4 Ho bisogno di sei biglietti. Ci sono posti non fumatori?
5 Speriamo di non avere problemi con il motore.
6 Non mi piace l'Internet. È difficile. Credo di essere troppo vecchio/a.
7 Non capisco. Può parlare più lentamente, per favore?
8 Fa caldo e c'è molta gente qui. Andiamo al lago.
9 Un'ora con lei mi fa venire il mal di testa.
10 C'è un autobus al semaforo. Dove va?
11 La carta di credito è sparita. Dobbiamo telefonare alla polizia.
12 Facciamo così: prima compriamo la Ferrari per me e dopo una T-shirt per Lei.
13 Mi piace quest'auto, però l'altra era meglio.
14 Abbiamo solo un litro di benzina e non c'è un benzinaio fino a Napoli.
15 Mi piace il sole e mi piace la pioggia. Tutti e due mi piacciono.
16 Pronto. Siamo a venti chilometri da Pisa. C'è un meccanico?
17 Scusi, può aiutarmi, per favore? Non conosco Roma. Dov'è la stazione?
18 La strada principale? Non è difficile se prende il metro.
19 Dove sono? Cosa hanno fatto? Non mi piace aspettare.
20 Veniamo dal binario diciassette. Dov'è Mario?

YOUR SCORE: ___ %

Week 6: Test your progress

1 Scriviamo molti e-mail perché abbiamo un computer nuovo.
2 Salve, posso aiutare? La sua borsa è sparita? Dove può essere?
3 Chi sa il numero del suo telefonino? Mi dispiace, non lo so.
4 Come va? Sono contento che non fuma più.
5 Vorrebbe vedere Bologna? È una città grande.
6 Non mi piace gennaio. C'è neve e spesso fa molto freddo.
7 C'è un chiosco laggiù. Desidera qualcosa da bere?
8 Perché non hanno telefonato? Abbiamo aspettato fino a ieri.
9 Prendo il libro. Dice che è interessante.
10 Credo che l'aeroporto è sempre aperto, giorno e notte.
11 È importante sapere quanto ha comprato il cliente.
12 Ha visto il giornale inglese? Non mi piace la foto. È brutta!
13 Ha detto che ha il raffredore. Spera di venire domani.

14 Un appartamento vicino al centro è caro in Italia?

15 Dobbiamo lavorare tutti e due. Tre bambini e due bambine costano molto.

16 Vado a Natale. Preferisco dicembre per le vacanze invece di luglio.

17 Conosciamo Marcello molto bene. Le piace?

18 Può darmi il cane? È piccolo ma simpatico. Cosa mangia?

19 Sua madre è qui. Non parla italiano.

20 Non lo sa? Le riparazioni costano cinquecento euro.

21 Devo passare al Bankomat. Ho bisogno di soldi.

22 Mi dispiace, ma **Instant Italian** è finito adesso.

YOUR SCORE: ___ %

Week 6: Say it simply

1 ...Scusi, ho un grande problema. Forse è vino rosso ma non sono certa. Siamo all'hotel solo fino a domani. Andiamo a Verona alle sette. Lo può fare per stasera per favore?

2 Pronto. Buongiorno, sono Kate Walker. Telefono dall'aeroporto. Sono stata nella camera 22 per tre giorni. Mi dispiace ma ci sono delle mie cose nella camera e come ho detto siamo adesso all'aeroporto e andiamo a Birmingham. Può aiutarmi per favore? L'hotel sa dove sono (vivo) a Birmingham. Molte grazie.

Week 6: Spot the keys

1 It depends when you are going. Normally it takes 20 minutes. But if there is a lot of traffic and there is a queue on the bridge, it takes at least 35 minutes. You can read the price on the meter. It will be between 20 and 25 euros.

2 They had of course been in... *England!*

how to use the flash cards

The **Flash cards** have been voted the best part of this course! Learning words and sentences can be tedious but with flash cards it's quick and good fun.

This is what you do

When the **Day-by-day guide** tells you to use the cards cut them out. There are 22 **Flash words** and 10 **Flash sentences** for each week. Each card has a little number on it telling you to which week it belongs. So you won't cut out too many cards at a time or muddle them up later on.

First try to learn the words and sentences by looking at both sides. Then, when you have a rough idea, start testing yourself – that's the fun bit. Look at the English, say the Italian, and then check. Make 'correct', 'wrong' and 'don't know' piles. When all cards are used up, start again with the 'wrong' pile and try to whittle it down until you get all of them right. You can also play it 'backwards' by starting with the Italian face-up.

Keep the cards in a little box or put an elastic band around them. Take them with you on the bus, the train, to the hairdresser's or the dentist's.

If you find the paper too flimsy, photocopy the words and sentences onto card before cutting them up. You could also buy some plain card and stick them on or simply copy them out.

The 22 **Flash words** of each lesson are there to start you off. Convert the rest of the **New words** to **Flash cards**, too. It's well worth it!

> **Flash cards for Instant learning:**
> **Don't lose them – use them!**

2 abbastanza	**2** un po'
2 male	**2** quanto
2 va bene	**2** la prima colazione
2 c'è	**2** diritto
2 qualcosa	**2** solo
2 il conto	**2** troppo

a little **2**	enough **2**
how much **2**	bad **2**
breakfast **2**	all right, ok **2**
straight on **2**	there is **2**
only **2**	something **2**
too, too much **2**	the bill **2**

2	oi	**2**	qui
2	a si tra	**2**	a destra
2	men	**2**	il marito
2	può	**2**	i servizi
3	oggi	**3**	dobbiamo
	tutto	**3**	dopo

here `2`	**then** `2`
(on the) right `2`	**(on the) left** `2`
the husband `2`	**less** `2`
the toilets `2`	**you can, he/she/it can** `2`
we must `3`	**today** `3`
after, afterwards `3`	**all** `3`

3	3
fino a	quando
3	3
più tardi	pezzo
3	3
ieri	vicino
3	3
lo stesso	questo
3	3
francobolli	comprare
3	3
credo	ho comprato

3	3
when	until
3 piece	**3** later
3 near	**3** yesterday
3 this	**3** the same
3 to buy	**3** stamps
3 I have bought	**3** I believe

3 chi	**3** aperto/a
3 la farmacia	**3** niente
3 vorrei	**3** non importa
4 qualcuno	**4** perché?
4 un appuntamento	**4** benissimo!
4 l'uscita	**4** davanti a

3 open	**3** who
3 nothing	**3** the pharmacy
3 it doesn't matter	**3** I would like
4 why, *also*: because	**4** someone
4 excellent!	**4** an appointment
4 in front of	**4** the exit

4 stasera	**4** che
4 dietro a	**4** su
4 nessuno	**4** meglio
4 certo	**4** posso
4 come	**4** una cosa
4 conosco	**4** un bicchiere

4	4
that, *also*: what?	tonight
4	**4**
on	behind
4	**4**
better	nobody
4	**4**
I can	sure, certain
4	**4**
a thing, matter	like, as *also*: how?
4	**4**
a glass	I know

4	4
con lui	dice

4	4
un cane	dolori

5	5
biglietto	aspettare

5	5
presto	fermata

5	5
altro/a	sparito/a

5	5
semaforo	caldo/a

4	4
he/she says	with him

4	4
pains	a dog

5	5
to wait	ticket

5	5
stop	quick, quickly

5	5
gone, disappeared	other

5	5
warm, hot	traffic light

5	**5**
pioggia	benzina
5	**5**
dare/dato	…mi piace
5	**5**
più	strada principale
5	**5**
tutti e due	vecchio/a
5	**5**
venire	contento/a
5	**5**
il problema	capisco

5 petrol	5 rain
5 I like…	5 to give/ given
5 main road	5 more
5 old	5 both
5 pleased, happy	5 to come
5 I understand	5 the problem

5 proibito	**5** pieno/a
6 Salve!	**6** città
6 aeroporto	**6** a Natale
6 libro	**6** appartamento
6 le riparazioni	**6** laggiù
6 la neve	**6** lo so

5	5
full	forbidden

6	6
town	Hello!

6	6
at Christmas	airport

6	6
apartment, flat	book

6	6
down there	the repairs

6	6
I know it	the snow

6	6
mai	vedo
6	6
conosciamo	fanno
6	6
invece (di)	meraviglioso/a
6	6
spesso	la nave
6	6
la madre	ha detto
6	6
l'aeroporto	la famiglia

6	6
I see	never, ever
they do	we know
wonderful	instead (of)
the ship	often
he/she said	the mother
the family	the airport

Buongiorno, sono… 1

un momento per favore… 1

Andiamo a Firenze. 1

Venezia è molto bella. 1

Lavoro a Londra. 1

per la mia ditta 1

Ho bisogno di molti soldi. 1

Adesso siamo in vacanza. 1

Abbiamo una casa. 1

Sono stato/stata in Italia. 1

Good morning, I am…

1

one moment, please…

1

We go/Let's go to Florence.

1

Venice is very beautiful.

1

I work in London.

1

for my company

1

I need a lot of money.

1

We are on holiday now.

1

We have a house.

1

I was/have been in Italy.

1

Ha una camera? 2

Dov'è la camera? 2

Quanto costa? 2

a che ora 2

Vorremmo andare a Roma. 2

alle otto e mezza 2

È troppo caro. 2

C'è un bar qui? 2

qualcosa da mangiare 2

il conto per favore 2

Do you have a room? 2

Where is the room? 2

How much does it cost? 2

at what time 2

We would like to go to Rome. 2

at half past eight 2

It is too expensive. 2

Is there a bar here? 2

something to eat 2

the bill, please 2

Mi dispiace. **3**

Dobbiamo andare. **3**

Vorrei fare spese. **3**

Devo passare al Bankomat. **3**

fino a quando **3**

C'è un negozio? **3**

Non importa. **3**

Ho comprato troppo. **3**

È molto simpatico. **3**

vicino alla posta **3**

I am sorry. **3**

We must go. **3**

I want to go shopping. **3**

I must go to the Bankomat. **3**

until when **3**

Is there a shop? **3**

It doesn't matter. **3**

I have bought too much. **3**

He is very nice. **3**

near the post office **3**

C'è qualcuno. 4

Non ha detto. 4

la settimana prossima 4

davanti alla porta 4

dietro alla chiesa 4

Non abbiamo tempo. 4

Andiamo a mangiare. 4

Vado con lui. 4

Mi aiuti per favore. 4

Come si dice in italiano...? 4

There is someone. 4

He did not say. 4

next week 4

in front of the door 4

behind the church 4

We don't have time. 4

We are going to eat. 4

I('ll) go with him. 4

Help me, please. 4

How do you say in Italian...? 4

andata e ritorno

5

Mi dispiace, non capisco.

5

Può parlare più lentamente?

5

A che ora c'è un treno?

5

Sono molto contento.

5

Mi piace la Fiat.

5

Mi piace, perché è nuova.

5

Mi piacciono tutti e due.

5

Il vino non mi piace.

5

Si può fumare qui?

5

return (ticket) 5

I am sorry, I don't understand? 5

Can you speak more slowly? 5

At what time is there a train? 5

I am very happy. 5

I like the Fiat. 5

I like it because it is new. 5

I like both. 5

I don't like wine. 5

Can one smoke here? 5

Nessuno lo sa. 6

Non lo so. 6

Che cosa c'è? 6

Cosa ha detto? 6

Cosa fanno? 6

Come va? 6

Non vedo… 6

Non c'è niente. 6

Non sono mai stato. 6

Andiamo da un amico. 6

Nobody knows it. **6**

I don't know it. **6**

What is it? / What is there? **6**

What did he say? **6**

What are they doing? **6**

How are you? **6**

I do not see… **6**

There is nothing. **6**

I have never been. **6**

We are going to a friend's. **6**

This is to certify
that

....

has successfully completed
a six-week course of

Instant Italian

with .... *results*

Elizabeth Smith

Date   *Instructor*